"Darling, Call the Coast Guard, We're on Fire Again!"

"Darling, Call the Coast Guard, We're on Fire Again!"

AND OTHER TALES OF LIVEABOARD LIFE

Catherine Dook

TouchWood Editions

TouchWood Editions are an imprint of Horsdal & Schubart Publishers Ltd. Victoria, BC, Canada.

Cover and book design by Public Art & Design, Victoria, BC.
Cover illustration by Pat McCallum, Victoria, BC.
Layout by Rossi McDonald, Victoria, BC.

We acknowledge the support of The Canada Council of the Arts for our publishing program. We also wish to acknowledge the financial support of the Government of Canada through the Book Publishing Industry Development Program (BPDIP) for our publishing activities. We also acknowledge the financial support of the Province of British Columbia through the British Columbia Arts Council.

This book is set in Garamond.
Printed and bound in Canada by Friesens, Altona, Manitoba.

National Library of Canada Cataloguing in Publication Data

Dook, Catherine, 1954-
  Darling, call the Coast Guard, we're on fire again, and other tales of liveaboard life

  ISBN 0-920663-81-8

  1. Dook, Catherine, 1954- 2. Boats and boating--Anecdotes. 3. Boats and boating--Humor. I. Title.
GV777.3.D66 2001   797.1'02'07   C2001-911349-8

BRITISH
COLUMBIA
ARTS COUNCIL
Supported by the Province of British Columbia

Printed and bound in Canada

To John

Acknowledgments

Many of these stories originally appeared in *South Cowichan Life*, *The Boat Journal* and *Nor'westing* magazines.

Thank you to Tina Knott, who first published me, and to Joe Pyke, who published me *and* paid me cash.

Thank you to my neighbours — we love you; my husband, an unending source of material; my extended family — if everybody buys a book, I could have a best-seller; and my wonderful children, who put up with all my whingeing, grizzling and complaining as I learned to sail (sort of), cook on a diesel stove (sort of) and dodge drips from the deckhead (haven't managed that one yet).

Thank you to Pat Touchie and Marlyn Horsdal of TouchWood Editions — you said "yes" to publishing this book.

And special thanks to all my readers, past and present — you laughed at my jokes.

Catherine Dook

Contents

Introduction

"So what made you decide to leave the Arctic?" asked my neighbour.

"Have you ever been there?" I asked.

"No."

"I didn't think so," I said.

We were sitting in the main saloon of the *Inuksuk*, a 44-foot ferrocement ketch moored at Cowichan Bay.

"The Arctic was a wonderful place to grow up. I was a little girl in Churchill, Manitoba, a teenager in Yellowknife, Northwest Territories, and an adult teaching in Kugluktuk, Nunavut. All doors in Churchill open inward, you know."

"Why is that?" asked my neighbour.

"Because some mornings, you'd wake up, swing open the door, and there'd be a solid bank of snow staring at you with a couple of inches of daylight showing at the top. Dad would have to dig his way out to get to work."

A drip fell into my coffee cup. "I wish this rain would stop," I commented. "More coffee?"

"What did your father do for a living?"

"He was a bush pilot. My mother spent most of her life in prayer. Dad made the CBC National News once, when his

Norseman fell out of the sky near Frobisher Bay. He was found by chance — the pilot who picked him up was lost. When Dad climbed into the cockpit, the first words the pilot said were, 'Hey, Rocky — do you know how to get to Frobisher Bay?'"

An alarm went off and I ran for a flashlight to peer into the bilge. "Looks like fresh water," I said, "but I'm not in the mood to taste it. I think there's a problem with one of our water tanks, but at least we're not sinking."

"They call the Arctic the Land of the Midnight Sun," my neighbour observed.

"That's true," I said. "In July in Yellowknife you can read a newspaper on Main Street at midnight. You suffer sleep deprivation all summer, but your vegetables grow like trifids. In winter you turn the colour of the underbelly of a dead fish and Mr. Light Bulb is your friend. All winter it's the land of the noonday darkness. I don't recall ever going to school in daylight. The sun hadn't risen on my way there, and it had set on my way home."

"Goodness," said my neighbour. "And what did you eat?"

"I'm not saying we suffered, but our diet was inadequate. The first time I saw a piece of fresh fruit, I nearly went into vitamin overload, and when my Grade One teacher told us cows give milk, nobody believed her. We all knew milk is powdered."

"It sounds exciting."

"Kind of a dull day today," I said. "I think I'll light some candles and an oil lamp or two. Smell anything? I wonder if the milk's gone off. Our refrigerator gave out last year."

"Do you have any brothers or sisters?"

"Two younger sisters. Beth is the youngest. When she was in Grade One, Gwen and I were responsible for getting her to school in Churchill. There were six-foot drifts of snow across the road, and the only way Gwen and I could manage it was to roll her up the snow banks sideways and drop her down the other side. She was stuffed into her snowsuit like a little pork sausage, so she didn't suffer any lasting harm. Beth always was an awfully good sport."

"Do you remember the time the docks broke up?" my neighbour asked.

I laughed. "Yes," I said. "And the time they were so icy and tippy that I had to crawl to the boat in the dark with my bag around my neck."

"Do you miss your job up North?"

"Sometimes," I said. "I had my very own classroom, and I loved the kids. Inuit children raise their eyebrows when they mean 'yes' and wrinkle their noses to say 'no.' The first day of school, my kids asked me if they could go to the washroom, meaning 'Can we explore this brand-new school and get into mischief?' I gave them my best shocked, raised-eyebrows look of 'What a question! and before recess too,' and the entire class thought I'd said 'yes.' They left, and it took the principal and me half an hour to round them up. But I get to substitute teach here, while John plays boats, so all is not lost."

"So how did you meet John?"

"I was teaching in Kugluktuk. John had been a folder of pink bloomers for the Hudson's Bay Company, a social worker, an adult educator and an art gallery owner. He spoke Inuktitut — a rarity among Englishmen. I was tough, resolutely independent and long-distance mum to my handicapped son. John was warm, funny and father to five adult children. He talked to me exactly as if I were a not-very-smart grandchild, and when he showed me how to use the Photostat machine, he looked so happy I fell flat in love. He claims he married me because there was nowhere to run. The wind outside would slice the skin right off your face, and the dark and light were savage.

"We both loved the North, but I arrived on the scene halfway between John buying the *Inuksuk* in Cowichan Bay and taking early retirement to move on board. He had a dream of new horizons and a future filled with gentle breezes, hot sunshine and bare-breasted women swimming out to the boat. Naturally, having just married him, I wasn't prepared to let a real husband slip through my fingers, and I was determined to supervise any baring of breasts. So I came with him. I'd never been on a boat in my life. Bush planes in winter, a canoe in spring — paddling through ice floes — and a dogsled once, but never a boat. It's been quite an experience, living aboard. You know, I think I might write a book."

"You should write a book about the Arctic," said my neighbour.

"I did," I said. "My father said if I published it, he'd be the first to sue me. This would be the other book."

John came down the companionway ladder carrying tools. "I've nearly finished that jib," he said proudly. "Hullo, neighbour! Hullo, Catherine!"

"Darling," I said, and I kissed him. "Do you know any lawyers?"

"Lawyers?" he said thoughtfully. "I don't think so..."

Ahoy the *Inuksuk*

THESE ARE THE adventures of the vessel *Inuksuk*. Our mission: to boldly go where no woman in her right mind would venture unless there were a man involved, to seek out new experiences, to navigate through the ways dressed for work in a skirt and pantyhose, and to finish fixing things that break down on board before we spend our life savings.

I'm a liveaboard. I wasn't always. I used to be a nice Arctic girl. I knew lots about snow and frostbite. I could pick blueberries and swat mosquitoes at the same time. I was a good sport when I sank into muskeg past my ankles. After years of camping I developed a passionate fondness for upholstery and plumbing.

My southern adventure began two years ago when I married John. Finding a husband in my forties was a feat that stunned and amazed my friends and family. Imagine my shock, too. So as we lay snuggled together on the couch, the Arctic wind slamming into the north wall and howling its way in great gasping swooshes around the building, John said, "I'd rather rust than freeze. I want us to live on board the *Inuksuk* together and sail the Pacific."

I sighed and rubbed my nose against his neck. "Of course, darling. What's the pointy end called again?"

A year later John resigned his position in the Arctic and we journeyed to beautiful Cowichan Bay and the *Inuksuk*.

I stood in front of the galley diesel oven where I gazed in silence. "You're kidding," I said.

"Of course not," said John.

"Darling," I said, trying to be tactful. "It looks like a rusted, clapped-out piece of junk." "It works," he said defensively. "And besides, every good galley cook is known for the shininess of her stovetop. I'll let you borrow my belt sander after lunch."

I tried again. "John," I said, "Do you recall at our wedding reception when my best friend took you aside and advised you to not sail any place where there wasn't take-out? Do you remember how adorable you thought it was when I told you I once lived in an apartment for five months before I discovered the oven didn't work? My cooking is marginal with thousands of dollars worth of kitchen equipment. I can't cook on this thing."

"That was then. This is now," said John. "What's for lunch?"

Lighting the oven involved setting fire to any paper that wasn't a chart and dropping it into a small sooty hole with the help of a flashlight and slamming the cast-iron lid on top before I set the lockers alight. There was no heat gauge, and I had to reach into a small, hot compartment to turn a burning-hot knob an unknown amount to the left to turn the heat down. My oven space was ten inches square, and the fan worked or didn't according to some agenda of its own.

"I want a shiny new propane one that works," I whined a week later. "I'll have to put off baking my more fragile pastries until I can figure out how to get the oven temperature

2

below 600 degrees, and even the lowly potato can take only so much abuse."

"Propane goes 'boom,' John said. "You told me yourself for the first twenty years of your adult life you thought the smoke alarm was a kitchen appliance. Diesel's safe. What's for lunch?"

I had hoped that a week of charcoal would resign him to eating out or spending thousands on an oven big enough for TV dinners.

One of John's most endearing characteristics is that he will eat nearly anything. He thinks beans on toast is a balanced meal. So I persevered with a will, a belt sander, and pages torn out of the *National Enquirer.*

By Christmas I had covered myself with glory. My tour de force was Christmas dinner for four, managed with the help of a small, deboned turkey. I was just able to fit the turkey and an enormous yam into the oven. I boiled potatoes, veggies and cranberry sauce on the stovetop, and even improvised some stuffing and plum pudding in the microwave.

The following summer I put down pounds and pounds of jam on a little two-burner electric stovetop, intoxicated with the thrill that I was able to get my hands on ten pounds of blueberries without having to swat a single mosquito.

I had finally resigned myself to the cooking arrangements on board the *Inuksuk.* Now if only I could remember what the pointy end was called.

The Maiden Voyage of the *Inuksuk* — or, How to Melt an Engine on the First Try

I T WAS A beautiful day — crisp and clear with a little snapping of the halyards. We'd planned this trip for weeks — no, months. We'd had the engine checked, we'd provisioned and we'd briefed the crew — me.

I was proud of myself. I'd graduated far beyond the raw novice who had been terrified to walk on the deck months earlier. I was miles in vocabulary past the woman who'd yelled at her husband, "Spring line? Spring line? Paris fashions? What in heaven's name do you mean, darling? Oh my God! We're going to hit the dock!" And "Round turn and two half hitches? A change of mind and two insincere commitments? Oh no! The boat's getting away!" And "Raise the mizzen? How can I raise something that's missing? Why is that sail flapping like that?" To my husband's credit, he doesn't yell at me.

I could read whole paragraphs of *The Sailor's Companion* and understand parts of it. I knew the difference between a genoa and a mainsail if I was given a minute to think about it, and I knew our boat was a 44-foot ferrocement ketch.

"You're the 'ketch,' John," I told him on the way past with an armload of life jackets.

"You may refer to me as 'captain,' he replied."You're not allowed to go all funny at sea."

We planned to go buddy sailing with a friend who is a fine sailor and terrific guy. Just before we pulled away, along came a very old friend of John's who entertained me while the men fuelled up.

"Last time John and I went out together, lucky thing the radio worked. We had to call the Coast Guard after the prop fell off. The Coast Guard nearly put his flares in their Hall of Fame. They'd never seen flares 30 years past the expiry date before. Yeah, every voyage with John is an adventure. Have a good trip."

His grinning face was the last one we saw as we pulled away.

"John," I said casually, "do we have flares?"

"Of course we do," he said.

"And these were — ah — purchased recently?"

"Well, yes," he said. "the Coast Guard confiscated the expired ones, and this prop doesn't have the electrolysis problem the prop on the other boat did. Besides, that was years ago."

"And our radio — does it work?"

"It works," he said defensively.

I was immediately suspicious. He'd said the same thing about our diesel oven when we'd first moved on board, and I'd spent a week trying to get it to register below 600 degrees. John is a wonderful man, but in his world, "it works" is a relative term.

We motored for a while, and then tacked down the bay towards Cape Keppel. I busied myself with my camera and the genoa. "Ready to come about, Captain," I learned to say jauntily. I started to think that all this was easier than it looked. John asked me to stop tacking for a while, so that I would not become too overworked on my first trip out, and he turned on the engine.

5

It purred along beautifully for an hour, and then suddenly stopped. When I ran below, a blanket of smoke greeted me. There was smoke pouring out of the engine room. "John, we're on fire," I yelled.

He came below and peeked into the engine room.

"Well, we're not exactly on fire," he said calmly.

The crew by this time was hysterical. "Not on fire? Not on fire? With that much smoke, how can you even tell? Where are the flares? Where's the fire extinguisher? Where's the radio?" I raced around the cabin for a while, waving a flare gun in one hand and a fire extinguisher in the other.

"Perhaps," John said gently, "you could raise our sailing buddy on the radio while I tend the sails."

In order to use the radio, I had to put down either the flare gun or the fire extinguisher. After a brief internal struggle, I put down the flare gun and grabbed the mike.

"This is the *Inuksuk*. This is the *Inuksuk*. I think we're on fire. This is a mayday. This is a may — Oh rats, John — the radio just died."

I went from hysteria to tears in a millisecond. I dragged myself up on the deck and presented a woebegone face to my husband, who was unperturbed.

"We're not on fire," he said. "We'll drop the sails and wave life jackets at our sailing partner. If we have to we'll drop anchor."

Our sailing buddy spotted our dropped sails and came steaming back to rescue us. "Don't feel bad, Catherine," he hollered cheerfully. "I've set fire to lots of engines."

He towed us back into our slip at Cowichan Bay, bless the man. I sat on the deck and knitted socks most of the way back, by this time able to see humour in the situation.

6

As it turned out, our Farymann engine possessed a plastic water-cooling jacket that actually melted. The alternator had shaken loose and fallen onto the water pump, thereby fouling up our water-cooling system. The engine overheated in a really big way and seized up. We had bent pistons, warped heads and a terrible mess.

"But all is not lost, darling," I said. "You have a wife with a job."

John may have had a hysterical crew, but ultimately, I was able to bring comfort. And it was still a beautiful day, after all.

Death Throes — The Grief
at Parting from the Old Engine

IN COWICHAN BAY, he who has a mechanical problem immediately attracts a crowd of knowledgeable bystanders who offer advice. This sounds like I'm making fun, but the truth is, these guys are experts, and an hour's consultation with the Cow Bay crowd is worth money. We'd been ignominiously towed into our slip, trailing smoke. This was a whole melted engine, so there were no less than six bystanders.

That John hadn't checked the oil immediately before leaving occasioned great mirth, but even so, there was a respectful procession of solemn-faced mourners below to view the deceased. They came out shaking their heads. "Looks bad," they all said.

"Can we fix it?" I asked hopefully.

"Maybe," was the terse reply. "New water jackets, fix you right up."

"How much?" I asked.

"Oh, new water jackets on a Farymann cost seven, eight hundred dollars."

"We could do that," I said, brightening.

"Plus installation," someone said from the back of the group. "Besides, you may need a new head or two. Fix you right up."

"How much?" I asked.

"Oh, new head on a Farymann costs one, two thousand dollars."

"We could do that," I said.

"Plus installation," said a man with a beard. "You may need a new engine. A little diesel would fix you right up."

"How much?" I asked.

"Oh, a new diesel engine of that size — ten, maybe twelve thousand dollars."

"Ten or twelve thousand dollars?" I exclaimed. "We don't want a new engine."

"Plus installation," said our sailing buddy. "And I ain't climbing into that hold on my knees to install a new engine. I'm too old and so are my knees. What you need is a little second hand diesel. Cost three, four thousand dollars. Fix you right up."

"What's the installation?" I asked.

"Oh, two, three thousand dollars."

"Well," I said, turning to John, "it's painful but not mortal. No beer for a year, no more movies or dinners out, cut back on steak and eat macaroni, no more wild sprees at Value Village throwing money around as if we were millionaires and we might just have it paid off by next summer. I want a shiny second hand one that works."

But John was optimistic that we'd be able to repair the Farymann. I kept silent, thinking that his loyalty to the Farymann was symbolic of fidelity in marriage, and that indications were he'd be as committed to me when I too was past my prime.

Extending the metaphor, I was thrilled at the depths John was prepared to plumb out of affectionate loyalty. The Farymann looked awful and smelled worse. It was blackened, and the bilge was filled with diesel sludge. The paint had all blistered off. I'm no mechanic, but my guess was that it was not a happy engine. I estimated, gauging from the condition of the engine, I'd be able to stop dyeing my hair and gain fifty pounds. I pulled out a bag of chips and began to munch happily.

"Whatever you say, dear," I said.

Son Rupert drove up from Alberta to administer last rites. He said holy words over the engine for three days and finally gave up.

"Catherine's right," he said. "You need a new engine."

I put down my chips. "I think I'll slip down to the drugstore while we can still afford hair dye, John," I said. "How do you feel about red?"

And so it came to pass, the passing of the old engine. Someone gave us two hundred dollars for the Farymann "as is," and I spent some of it on Ry-Krisp. Fixed me right up, and I didn't need to consult with anybody about it. Some things should be done secretly and in silence.

Cleaning the Bilge — Never Volunteer

A H, THOSE LONG, lazy, lingering summer days — days that slipped by us like a rudder sliding through foamy water — days we couldn't sail because we didn't have an engine.

There was a blackened hole where our Farymann used to be. Sometimes I'd peek into the engine room out of a sense of nostalgia, while John would wistfully smell the breeze and note wind direction. The bilge underneath was filled with unmentionable diesel-smelling sludge. Our marine mechanic humbly requested that we clean the bilge before he crawled into the engine room with bowed back to install the second-hand Isuzu engine for which we'd bartered away our life savings.

"He looks kind of grubby," I whispered to my husband. "Are you sure he knows what he's doing?"

"Best marine mechanic on the coast," John hissed back. "What'd you expect, a poster boy for Javex bleach? He installs engines, for heaven's sake."

I was dubious at first, then happy that our mechanic's standards extended to a clean bilge. "I'll take care of cleaning the bilge," I told John airily. "After all, how hard can it be?"

"It's a heavy job," said John. "Do you want some help?"

"Nonsense, darling," I said. "Leave the cleaning jobs to the family expert."

"How do you clean a bilge?" I asked my neighbour over mugs of coffee on the dock the next morning.

"Nothing to it," she replied. "You pour bilge cleaner into the bilge and the next time you go sailing the movement of the boat sloshes the bilge around and does all your work for you."

"Gee, it sounds so easy," I said, "And what's the procedure if you can't go sailing because you haven't got an engine?"

"Oh dear," she said, and turned a little pale. "It's a little more complicated then. You have to scrub." She finished her coffee and escaped to her boat as quickly as she could.

I started by pumping the bilge as far as I could pump it with a portable electric apparatus. To do this I had to kneel on an angled floor, lean partway around a corner and grope in the slimy depths of the bilge with one end of the hose and balance the other end in a large greasy bucket, while holding a lit flashlight in my teeth. With my elbow I connected two wires to make the bilge pump go.

"They didn't cover this in high school," I complained.

"What was that, Catherine?" asked John. "I can't understand you with that flashlight in your mouth."

"And six years of higher education didn't prepare me for this either," I snarled, spitting the flashlight on the floor and turning to glare at my husband.

"Put the flashlight back, darling," said John blithely. "You can't see in the dark. Are you having fun?"

"I would rather eat worms from a dead caribou's nose," I said loftily, and popped the flashlight back into my mouth.

I poured soapy water into the bilge and scrubbed with a long-handled brush, nearly standing on my head to get to the far reaches of the bilge and gasping for air. Bilge-slime extended up my arms and splashed me in the face.

"Taste it quick," said John with a smirk. "And tell me if it's salt or fresh."

I didn't condescend to reply. John and I took turns pumping, then sloshed and scrubbed some more. Bilge slime pooled around my knees and sucked at my feet. Suddenly stricken with one of those flashes of genius that come to the brilliant and the simple-minded alike, I stripped down to my underwear and scoured happily away, delighted that I wasn't going to get my clothes dirty. Hours later, the bilge was presentable, and after a shower, so were we.

When the marine mechanic, genius in grubby jeans that he was, came to install the engine, I was glad every time I saw his tired, smudged face, and I never again complained about the state of his wardrobe. He worked silently, stopping to comment only once that he was grateful he didn't have to install the engine while up to his knees in bilge water.

"You have Catherine to thank for that," said John generously.

"Can you still attain sainthood," I mused aloud, "when you complain the whole way there?"

The two men were too polite to answer me, but I thought I heard a faint chuckle from my husband.

Painting the *Inuksuk* —
Don't Volunteer for That Either

I T WAS A beautiful day. The sun shone, the wind blew and there was a restless stirring among the halyards, as if the *Inuksuk* was anxious to be off on the high seas.

"Yes, a beautiful day," said John. "Perfect for painting the deck."

"Painting the deck," I exclaimed. "Let's pack up some sandwiches and strawberries and a thermos of coffee and go for a sail. There's a dear."

"Nonsense," said my beloved. John was once in the British military and he is fond of painting things.

Over breakfast coffee on the dock I spoke to my neighbour. "A perfect day for sailing, and we're stuck here painting," I complained.

"But Catherine," she said. "People who own boats don't go sailing. They spend all their time painting and scraping and washing and scrubbing and repairing things that break down. The whole point of owning a boat isn't about sailing — it's spending your life savings and all your energy in repairing your boat. It's being broke and broken down nearly all the time."

"Sort of like being married to an alcoholic and not going to any parties?" I asked.

"No parties? You have the wrong attitude," she exclaimed. "Girl, this is FUN!" Then she laughed like a lunatic. "Have to go now — there's mildew under the bunk and I have to hunt it down and flush it out before lunch. Have a good time with your paintbrush."

I couldn't get sympathy from anyone.

"All right, I give up," I said to John. "Hand me a paintbrush."

"A paintbrush?" said John. "Don't be foolish. First we have to scrub the boat and put down tape. I plan to put silicone sand on the deck to make it non-slip."

"Tape?" I asked. "Are we painting more than one colour?"

"Well, yes," said John. "The hull is blue, so I thought cream for the sides of the deck and 'sunburst' for the top." He produced a can with a flourish. I eyed it dubiously.

"Darling," I said, "I hate to pull this 'girls know more about this than guys' stuff on you, but any female worth her salt who has graduated from Fabric and Dress 10 knows brown and blue don't go together."

"This isn't brown," he said proudly. "It's 'sunburst.'"

I value my marriage, so I kept silent.

The neighbours did not. By the time we were on our second coat, even John was calling it "diaper brown."

"It's exactly the colour of cat diarrhea," said one passerby. "In fact, just now I was walking down the dock and I nearly stepped…"

"Too much information," said John.

"Well," I said helpfully, "on the up side, anyone who is seasick on the deck won't stain the paint. It's exactly…"

"Too much information," said John. "I like it."

"Hey, John!" yelled one neighbour. "That's the worst shade of brown I've ever seen in my life."

"It wouldn't be so bad," murmured his wife politely. "But in combination with the navy-blue hull…" Her voice trailed off and she shuddered significantly.

One person liked it. "I like it," said our marine mechanic positively.

"He likes it," said John.

"Darling," I said, "not only did we buy the paint from him, we've given him eight thousand dollars for our new engine. If you gave me eight thousand dollars I'd like it too."

"Well," said John, "if you want to change it, you'll have to repaint it."

"I like it," I said. "But next time, John, when you shop for paint, will you let me tag along? I bet the neighbours would appreciate it."

As the summer progressed, it struck me that some obscure chemistry was occurring between our ferrocement boat, the sun and our new "diaper brown" paint. I'd carefully shaken the silicone sand on foot by foot, crouched under the hot sun, and though I disliked the colour of the paint, I had no intention of redoing the chore unless I absolutely had to.

"What's with this paint?" I asked my husband.

"Well, the rule of thumb is that the more expensive the paint, the faster it peels off a ferrocement boat," he said.

"Let me understand this," I said. "Not only do we have the worst colour combination on the B.C. Coast, but we're going to have a tatty boat on top of it?"

"Well no," said John. "We'll repaint the boat next year. I'll let you do the hull, too, if you're a good girl."

At least he's tidy.

Housewives Afloat

FINDING PHYSICAL AND mental stimulation for the live-aboard housewife is not much of a challenge. There's always something interesting to do and see. Summer evenings will find the men of the dock gathered in little clusters, discussing such boring topics as boat engines and where you can buy boat parts cheap.

"And only four hundred and fifty dollars," says my husband, dramatically flinging a tarp from on top of a rusted hulk.

There are murmurs of admiration from the crowd. Such direct questions as "Does it work?" are considered the height of bad manners.

The women, on the other hand, boast a far-flung range of topics that encompass boat lore and our husbands. The combinations and permutations are endless fodder for conversation. At evening consultations we discuss which husbands notice when you use their toothbrush to clean corners, the uses of vinegar to remove salt stains and how to avoid having your husband do something as lunatic as go offshore. "Easy," said one woman. "I just wouldn't go."

We've discussed the Christmas the deboned turkey crashed around inside the oven so much that the cook's in-laws thought she'd beaten the bird to death, and the time the dinner guests all had to leave because everyone was seasick and the cook wouldn't get out of the head. I've complained that my husband's wardrobe favourites are thrift-store rejects, and I've elaborated on a particular see-through T-shirt and a pair of shorts the same ghastly "diaper brown" shade as our deck. My neighbour has complained her husband gets putty on all her steak knives and uses her favourite hand-embroidered dishtowels as grease rags. One evening we gathered around a milk carton and decided which of our husbands had symptoms of Tourette's syndrome.

"Short attention span? Repetitive behaviour? Sounds like mine."

"Mine has nervous tics and a short temper."

"You know, these messages on the sides of milk cartons are a real public service. I'd have just thought he was eccentric because he had to watch 'The Simpsons' every night and got so hostile and excited every time I wanted to use the fire extinguisher."

We've also discussed the role of "Xena, Warrior Princess" in our marriages. "My first clue should have been our first kiss. His eyes rolled so wildly I thought he was excited, but I realize now I was just blocking his view of Xena. I married him on a day Xena wasn't on TV on the theory he'd be more likely to show up."

"I just hand my husband a towel to wipe the saliva off his chin."

"My husband claims he watches the program to get lingerie ideas for anniversary presents. When I told him I would find little practical application for metal underwear, he was so disappointed that I dropped the subject."

18

One neighbour and I decided we were going to exercise ourselves down to glamorous thinness by Christmas, so after supper we'd walk up the hill and down the road. Every evening you'd see us — two fat ladies collapsed into a telephone pole at the top of the hill, gasping for breath like landed dolphins. We didn't lose much weight, but we exchanged all manner of useful and entertaining information.

I learned why upholstery turns mouldy and the practical uses of Styrofoam under bunks. I learned that if you hit a rock and tear out the underside of your boat, the procedure is to rip up the floorboards and stuff the seat cushions in the holes. Fast. Our boat is ferrocement; I've been advised to remember where the life raft is or cut the line to the dinghy. I learned where you can buy fresh berries cheap, and I learned who on the dock fixes computers. But from my friendships I have learned some things are paramount: Murphy is on board as crew, the Captain may not be perfect but he's still the Captain, and a sense of humour and a lot of love will take you a long way. Maybe even offshore. This is what I have learned.

Crewmember Murphy

I WANTED TO see Cape Keppel up close. We hadn't made it there, and it was all Murphy's fault. Murphy is the invisible crewmember who, according to local folklore, causes things to go wonky for those who are afloat. My neighbour explained it to me: "You come home and your hot-water tank has sprung a leak and your floorboards are floating. Murphy. Your tank heats and leaks and heats and leaks and the bilges pump and pump, and your bilges are clean enough to lick and your boat's nearly sunk. Murphy. Hit a rock, lose your dinghy, nearly sink the boat with inflow along the prop shaft, drag your anchor...all Murphy. I know him well and I bet you will, too."

On our first trip out we melted the engine just short of the Cape and our eyes were too full of smoke to take in its vast natural beauties. Preoccupied with what I was sure was imminent death on the rocks or by suffocation, the loss of 100% of our family assets and later, embarrassment at being towed home trailing smoke, I was unable to appreciate the serene majesty of the view. Coughing slightly, we lowered our hat brims and counted ourselves glad that we didn't meet any boaters we knew. Murphy.

The second time out, we were intent upon glory. We entered the Great Cowichan Bay Basement-Suite Race. Intoxicated with the possession of a brand-new $8,000 engine and six bottles of apple cider, we borrowed a crew from our neighbours (who with John did the actual sailing) and we tacked like mad things up the bay in a dead heat with six — count 'em — six (or maybe it was five) other boats. We came in third and won a prize I refer to as our "$8,000 T-shirt." My, but the boats looked pretty with their sails up. Trouble was, at Separation Point we luffed in a circle and floated back wing-on-wing, too frantic in our lust to be third and to yell insulting taunts at our friends to continue further up the Bay. "Hey there — want a tow?" we hollered, and "That guy in first place has too many sails. Make him cut off one of his masts." And I still hadn't had a close look at Cape Keppel.

The third time John and I left Cowichan Bay, we joked a little as we left the dock. "Let's make Cape Keppel," we said, confident that our new engine and the prize winning and now sober crew (me) should have no difficulty. Last time we'd docked, hadn't I leaped over an expanse of ocean nearly a yard wide onto the dock to pull the stern line and guide the boat in? Hadn't John once been mentioned in *Reader's Digest* the time he was rescued off Great Slave Lake? Weren't we practically experts? We set off with a jaunty angle to our shoulders, bound for — dare I say it — a destination beyond Cape Keppel — Fulford Harbour. But it was not to be. We became respectfully silent as we neared the Cape. Suddenly, such a banging and racket came from the engine as caused our eyes to bulge from their sockets.

"An airlock," moaned my husband.

"Murphy," I exclaimed. "Murphy's on board." My husband and I are a perfect blend of nautical science and sailor superstition. John grabbed the radio to raise our buddies, who had been our crew on the Basement-Suite race. Our friend thought we might have some bad fuel, but his wife's diagnosis concurred with mine.

"It's Murphy for sure," she said. "I recognized him right away. He's been on board our boat for years."

Perhaps the least said about the trip back the better. It was the day of the Cowichan Bay Sailing Regatta. We blundered directly into a massed bank of mad, intent, world-class expert racing sailors, who waved greetings at us and shouted cries of encouragement. At least I thought that's what they were doing. We were going the wrong way down a freeway at rush hour with a crippled engine, a crew who was too terrified to open her eyes and a captain with nerves of steel. All the blood had drained from his face, but he didn't faint and he didn't hit anybody. When we docked I crawled off the deck on my hands and knees and offered thanks to God. I didn't offer thanks to Murphy. All curiosity about Cape Keppel drained out of me for at least a week. I wonder what it's like there?

Titanic vs Inuksuk

"CATHERINE," SAID JOHN, "Do you remember the time I was building the hard dodger and I sent you to the lumber store to get a tin of paint any colour but white and you came back with a tin of white paint?"

"Yeah? So?" I said. "Anybody can make a mistake."

"Well, I'm finally giving in. I'd like you to go to the video store and rent *Titanic*. Let's see how you do." I was wildly excited. At last — I'd get to see the blockbuster that made our melted engine look like we'd done it on purpose. John has refused to see the movie in the theatre. He said that as a boat owner, paying that much money to watch a boat taking on that much water made him nervous. "Besides," he said, "the hero is a puppy and grossly overrated."

"Everyone knows the mature man is more attractive to a discerning woman," I said. "Now let's watch."

"Are there any aliens in this movie?" asked John. "I like aliens."

We enjoyed the movie, but I was left with some questions about the contrast between our way of life and the luxurious living on board the *Titanic*.

Why don't I own any evening gowns like Kate Winslet's for dinners on board our boat? As we elegantly dine on beans and wieners à la *Inuksuk*, should not my delicately pearlized shoulders gleam in the glow of our 40-watt bulbs? Unfortunately, silk fabrics wrinkle in our lockers, and there is insufficient room on board to maintain a wardrobe of evening wear. Otherwise we'd be delighted to dress for dinner.

And where is our cultivated, stylish conversation? My husband and I spend our evenings speculating which of our systems is going to break down next.

"I think the impeller on the head is about due to go," I say.

"Naw," says John, "my bet is the diesel oven fan — listen to it squeak."

"Did you test the bilge alarm today?" I ask.

"Have you checked the battery levels?" asks my husband. "That 12-volt light looks a little dim. I wonder if our battery charger will hold out."

It's nearly as exciting as sinking.

Where are the elegant appointments of our boat? The crystal? The china? Do my "Old Country Roses" salt and pepper shakers (worth nearly thirty dollars) count? How does my Corelle Livingware stack up against the fine china on board the *Titanic*? And most important of all, would my dear husband, who before we were married ate stew out of a tin, even notice? The answer to this question is an unqualified no.

Where are the attractive lovers racing through our boat hand-in-hand? There isn't room on board the *Inuksuk* to run together and the only rushing we do is to the head. John doesn't sketch my recumbent nude figure as I recline languorously wearing nothing but the necklace he gave me

24

last Christmas. He eats Weetabix wearing his housecoat and watches TV.

Where is our discreet, well-trained troop of servants? Some nights I would like to have a skilled chef fry the pork chops and boil the potatoes, and we would both appreciate having a deckhand scrape the scum off the bottom of the dinghy.

Where is our fine art? Our Van Goghs? Our Monets? We, too, encourage young artists, but our original crayon sketches were done by our grandchildren.

And where is the passionate love affair? I look over at my husband.

"Am I beautiful?" I ask.

"Absolutely, and so thin," he says.

You see? Everyone knows the mature man is more attractive to a discerning woman. I return the video to the store, grateful for what we have. There are no icebergs in Cowichan Bay, we're still afloat and I'm married to John. "Come back with anything except a musical," he says. So I rent *Evita*.

Murphy on Boat Repair

WHENEVER YOU SEE two liveaboards talking to each other, they're discussing what broke down on board their boats that week. There's a never-ending list of things that have to be tended, maintained, inspected and repaired. To the novice, it can be a bewildering experience. However, by dint of a careful study of Murphy's Law, I have determined a series of rules governing boat repairs.

1. He who first moves on board is faced with a daunting list of things that don't work.
2. Pumps, electrical switches, galley fixtures and water valves break down at the rate of about two a week for the first year.
3. He who repairs even at an incredible rate of speed has about a year before the first repairs have to be completely redone.
4. Never assume that the source of heat that ran like a Rolls Royce last spring will even start up in the fall.
5. Your freezer is big enough to hold two or three bodies, but it doesn't freeze.

6. Regular maintenance increases the probability that you will find a serious problem with one of your systems.
7. The head is most likely to completely expire in the middle of the night.
8. The probability of something breaking down is exponentially related to the height of the fever your husband is running.
9. The broken pump that looks like a plastic toy costs two hundred and fifty dollars, plus tax.
10. The first mate is expected to do the "prep" work. Prep work usually involves bilge slime.
11. Breakdowns are the fault of the crew.
12. If your engine is going to baulk, it will be in the middle of a channel in the most adverse possible weather conditions.
13. Your husband is too embarrassed to call the Coast Guard, even if the boat is on fire.
14. Your neighbours are an invaluable source of information about repairs — over the years their boat has completely broken down too.
15. The first mate who develops a sense of humour halfway through a repair is subject to instant demotion.

With the assistance of these simple guidelines, anyone should be able to navigate their way through the repairs on their boat. Fortunately, there are compensations for the liveaboard. During rainstorms we sit tucked up in the main saloon, sipping hot coffee and listening to a blues CD counterpoint the raindrops pattering on the deck and, "John! Put that flashlight down. It's only a drip, for heaven's sake!" I guess there's another rule: the husband who starts out as a reluctant repairer is obsessive within weeks.

We are optimistic that some day our boat will be "done," but when, with glowing eyes and trembling lips, we tell our neighbours of this dream, they nearly fall into the ocean laughing. So we've stopped telling people. That's the very last rule.

The Great Carburetor Controversy

"SOME PEOPLE ARE high on life. We're high on diesel fumes," I said.

"I don't smell anything," said my husband.

"But John," I said, "you think my cooking smells good, too, even when I slip up and it's flambé."

"Yum. French cooking," said John. "Can we have some of that tonight?"

"I'm serious, John. The boat's going to be flambé if we don't do something about our diesel leak. I swear, that stove carburetor dribbles like a St. Bernard."

"Put a bowl under it," said John.

"Fix it, darling," I said, and I meant it. "I go to work smelling of "eau de diesel" and my co-workers are ready to report me to Environment Canada. They'll get us anyway if they see a spreading oil slick around the boat."

John's face took on the agonized expression of a man trapped between a nattering wife and a dirty job. "Oh, all right," he said finally.

First stop was the marine store, where we negotiated for a new carburetor.

"A hundred and fifty dollars?" exclaimed John. "It's only an old diesel stove, for goodness sake!" He put his debit card back into his wallet. "It's going to take me all day just to figure out how to fix the carburetor onto this bracket. And I don't recognize the carburetor. It's new. The stove's old. It won't fit." He turned to go.

I grabbed his arm. "Please John," I begged, "I want the leak fixed."

He caved in and bought the carburetor.

Being a sensible woman, I spent the day of the great carburetor switch investigating thrift stores. At lunch I phoned home.

"The new carburetor doesn't work," he said. "I bought a bunch of fittings and went out for coffee just so I could ask advice up at the café, and everyone agrees it's the only carburetor we can get and that our stove is too old for it."

"Rats," I said. "What can we do?"

"We?" he said, "I'm the one doing all the work."

"Shopping is a terrible strain on the system. I've heard you say so yourself," I said. "My part of the job will be to shop and offer sympathy. What's your plan?"

"The only thing I can do is put the old carburetor back on and hope the marine store will take the new one back." I rang off thoughtfully. From the sound of John's voice, I'd have to visit three more thrift stores.

Later in the afternoon I returned home. John was sitting quietly in the corner. The main saloon was dark and the boat was cold.

"What's wrong?" I asked.

"Now the old carburetor doesn't work," he said.

"Oh dear," I said.

We hired a smart person to start the stove and John perked up considerably after the boat was warm and the marine store agreed to take back the carburetor.

"Darling," I said, "I'm sorry. It was my idea to replace the carburetor, and the new carburetor couldn't possibly work, and then the old carburetor wouldn't work either after you'd gone to all the trouble of reinstalling it, and we had to pay someone to jump start the system and we still don't know why it didn't work or how we fixed it. I'm sorry." There was silence. "Darling," I said, "I notice you're not saying, 'That's all right, dear. It's not your fault at all.'"

"That's right, dear," said John. "I didn't say that." We snuggled together in the main saloon and sipped our mugs of coffee in contented companionship. Funny thing — I couldn't smell any diesel at all.

Going Offshore

WHEN WE MOVED on board, it was with the intention of eventually going offshore. Naturally, I kept my ears and eyes open to find out as much about the experience as possible. John often handed me pertinent magazine articles or brought home interesting people with interesting stories to tell. I was quite daunted by some of the tales I heard, and I wondered if I would be able to live up to the reputation of the intrepid sailors who had gone before me.

My favourite story was the one about the woman whose husband was incapacitated after their boat rolled. She spat out a couple of teeth and climbed the mast with a knife clenched in her gums to cut the rigging and repair the sails. Halfway through the ordeal of sailing the crippled boat by herself across the Pacific, she discovered she was pregnant, and months later was delivered of a beautiful baby. I saw a photograph of the proud parents and their baby, and I was struck by how happy the mother looked and how nice her hair was. I felt intimidated. I'd never climbed a mast and I hoped I'd never have to. I couldn't sail even with a crew to help me, and if I became pregnant at sea, there would be a case of "man overboard." Furthermore, how did a liveaboard get such nice hair? I'm of sturdy stock, but not that sturdy. John points to this woman as someone I should emulate, but beside her I feel old, fat and cowardly. Men generally offer no sympathy. I heard about the couple who were demasted and their deck swept clean. The husband allegedly said, "I don't know why she's so upset about it. It only happened once."

John once brought home an old navy man who told a terrific story. "My Dad was a cook aboard a navy warship. When the ship sank off the coast of Africa, poor bugger didn't even get a chance to drown. The sharks got him. Civilians aboard. Women, too. They say you could hear the screams of the dying passengers all the way to…"

"More coffee, anyone?" I asked with a slight tremor in my voice. Later, I spoke with my husband.

"Darling," I said coaxingly, "we don't want to go to Africa, do we? Nasty continent, with large flying insects and poisonous snakes and large voracious sharks."

"Of course we do," said John. "You just don't want to go skinny dipping in the coastal waters, is all."

Another friend had an equally harrowing tale about the Philippines. "Pirates got me. I spent two hours with a submachine gun shoved in my mouth and a rifle cocked at each ear while they stripped my boat. They took everything that wasn't screwed down. But they let me live, and they left my boat afloat. I was really lucky."

"Lucky," I echoed with white lips. "Darling," I said later, "let's not go to the Philippines. I'm not fond of pirates."

"Neither am I," said John. "Take the federal government, for example…"

I wasn't being taken seriously. Maybe I could delay the process. "John," I said, "if we're going offshore, shouldn't one of us speak Spanish?"

"We already speak Spanish," said John. "Bueno! Taco! Ole! Besides, both of us have a little French, and that'll do." He eyed me narrowly. "My father had a saying. You can lead a fish to water, but you can't make it make hay. What's the matter? Don't you want to go offshore with me?"

"The way it stands now," I said, "if you're going to do something as foolhardy as go offshore, I'm coming with you to tell you what to do." I had doubts.

Later, we decided to make another lunge at Cape Keppel. We'd made several attempts to get there, but twice something nasty had happened to our engine. We had a new engine to test, and we were full of optimism. We toasted each other with coffee at the local café before we left. "Here's to a bug free trip," we said gaily, and we cast off with light hearts.

We glided out of our slip and headed for open water, the salt sea on our lips and the sun in our hair. The bow dipped gracefully, and the spray caught the sunlight. The wind whipped a little at the sails, but we stubbornly ran the engine, determined to test it to the max. Such an exhilarated feeling gripped me as we skimmed over the waves.

I held the helm steady while John gleefully played with his "toys" — our depth finder (registered us as a mile above sea level at one stage), our GPS ("GPS is for sissies," says one friend of John), and our radar, ("But it's daylight," I said to John). Seagulls squawked overhead and flashed past, the sun glinting off their wings. The wind whipped my hair.

I peered ahead.

"There it is!" I yelled, "The Cape, John — it's the Cape!"

I stared in wonder. There it loomed, as big a mountain as I'd ever seen, covered with great trees and rocks and dirt and well, it was beautiful. We'd spent a year trying to get four miles down the coast to Cape Keppel. We'd melted an engine and worked bugs through another. We'd repaired everything on the boat at least once, and we had become expert at maneuvering around our slip to the fuel dock. We'd become such practitioners of deferred gratification that we'd nearly forgotten the object was to go sailing. Past the Cape we could catch a glimpse of the open sea. There were tears in my eyes.

"John," I said, "I want to go offshore."

Seasick

WHEN I WAS in high school, I was in love with a boy we will call "Clayton." Clayton was the smartest and best looking boy in our school. Every three or four months he'd bestow a kindly word on me, so naturally I loved him dumbly and hopelessly from afar. Later, when I was at university, Clayton once came to visit another — prettier — friend of mine and included me in the group. Chattering excitedly, we went off to a Mr. Mike's for coffee and burgers. There was a low wall at the entrance. I hopped over it and turned back, waiting for the other two. There was my girlfriend, a healthy woman of 19, being solicitously assisted up the steps. She was limping slightly and leaning heavily on Clayton as if the mere sight of a little ice rendered her temporarily crippled. As I stood there in my size nine hiking boots, I could feel my passion for Clayton drain south. Love died at the moment I realized the man I adored was a credulous nitwit.

Twenty-five years later, the man to whom I am married, who is a nautical sort, doesn't expect vapours and prissy ways. Au contraire, John has been heard to speak with admiration of the competent way I can throw around fifty-pound containers of diesel fuel, and leap from a heaving boat onto a heaving dock. I hardly ever complain that I can't bake pies when it rains because my pie plate (and one of my good forks) is wedged under a beam to catch drips. I've been known to wash dishes up to my forearms in icy water, and trudge through the streaming rain carrying sacks of dirty laundry. I'm sure all this is very character forming, so I appreciate my husband's assistance in my development. However, I draw the line at seasickness. I see no merit in it.

The other day, it started to blow. I eyed the spaghetti sauce slopping in the pot. "I'll turn on the diesel oven for you," said John. "That pot is going to slide straight off the electric burner." He had a point. The diesel oven has a little metal harness around the top of the stove, perfect for catching pots before they slide onto the galley floor. I hung grimly on in the galley, observing the pots shifting uneasily about the stovetop. Stirring seemed superfluous, but I felt I was needed to steer the pots back to the hot spots on the stovetop. "John," I shouted over the noise in the rigging, "dinner is served." I maneuvered two slippery servings of spaghetti onto plates and slopped a helping of sauce on top. I passed a plate to John, noticing that his serving had slid precariously to the side of the plate. "Not an inspired menu choice for a blow," I commented, as I chased my spaghetti around my plate, and my plate around the galley table.

It was an hour later that I felt ill. John had left to join the group of murmuring men shaking their heads over the state of the docks. Some of the float homes were banging into each other, and people were needed to haul them into position. I tidied the galley and secured my Depression glass. I sat quietly on one side of the main saloon, stricken with a sudden thoughtfulness brought about by the status of my digestive tract. The boat was rolling from starboard to port. The cutlery was shifting uneasily in the drawers, and the cabin was waving wildly. I could hear the roaring of the wind, the slapping of the halyards, the "chink, chink" of the cutlery, and the terrible groaning as the boat heaved into the dock and ground the fenders to a pulp. Outside the men were shouting, and I heard a crash as two float homes struck each other. I ran to the companionway and climbed up the ladder. Outside, it looked chaotic. The docks were heaving and writhing like snakes, and the float homes and other boats seemed bent on throwing themselves into the docks and each other. It was dark, but there was an eerie glow in the air. I hailed my husband, who was on his way past to one of the float homes. "John," I yelled, "are the docks going to hold?"

"Oh, sure," he hollered.

"Are the mooring lines going to hold?" I yelled.

"Should do," he shouted.

"Am I going to hold?" I yelled.

"What's the problem?"

"I'm seasick and there's no horizon to look at."

"Go up to the café and take a rest," he yelled. I eyed the docks with trepidation. I'd seen friendlier charging polar bears. I swung myself to the deck and poised myself over the dock — there! The boat heaved sideways and the dock rose up to meet it. I jumped and landed uncertainly on the writhing dock. Staggering slightly, I made my way towards the ramp. Past me in the dark ran a local character dressed in a pair of shorts and a loud shirt. "It's a miracle," he yelled, "I can walk straight." I crawled up the ramp and lurched toward the café, haven of the queasy. There I sat slumped sideways in my chair until the hiccoughs passed. My stomach felt as murky as a septic tank in midsummer, and as unsettled as an in-law at a family reunion. I was incapable of even the contemplation of a cup of tea, and the happy exclamations of the patrons of the cafe nauseated me. As I sat in my chair clutching the edge of the table, my life seemed futile and happiness a mocking dream. I thought about going offshore for weeks, and the impossibility of escaping to a quiet dark restaurant in the middle of the Pacific, and a small agonized moan escaped my lips that ended prosaically in a belch. John bounced in through the doorway, banging the door behind him.

"How are you feeling?" he asked kindly, and I gazed dumbly at him in helpless gratitude. A faint shadowy memory of Clayton flashed across my mind. I rallied immediately. After all, didn't I pride myself on being a good sport?

"Darling," I said, "I feel fine," and arm in arm we made our way back to the boat. The *Inuksuk* was still throwing herself into the dock, but I and my stomach felt ready to try again. There are times when a little sympathy does wonders. As I snuggled next to John in the aft cabin, I wondered briefly if Clayton married someone as nice as I did. Then the boat rocked us to sleep.

Cleaning the Stove

"I THINK YOU should clean the diesel stove," said John. "Me?" I asked. "I have important things to do — like read *Rumpole of the Bailey* and eat crackers."

"Well," said John, "I may not always be here, and then you'll have to know how to do it."

"Oh, John," I said, putting down my book, "I don't want to think about the time you're not here."

"Oh, I didn't mean dead," said John, "I meant maybe up at the pub getting drunk." I snorted and put my book away. It looked as though John was determined to do chores.

"So, what's first?" I asked.

"Well, first you find the portable vacuum cleaner I bought at Value Village for six dollars — it's stowed in the locker opposite the head." I dug for a minute, flinging life jackets and gear aside with reckless abandon until I found it — a disreputable looking relic hidden under a survival suit. I held it out at arm's length, while the soot-smeared hose entwined itself around my clean jeans. I eyed it with distaste.

"This filthy thing?" I asked.

"Wear rubber gloves," said John, tossing me a pair. The gloves, too, had been used to clean the stove, and they were as sooty as the vacuum cleaner.

Thanks to my liberal use of the fall and winter Sears catalogue when lighting the stove, the firepot was full of ash and clinkers, and the chimney was choked with soot. It seemed only fair that I participate in the cleaning job, since I was largely responsible for the mess.

We pulled the top off the chimney and then pulled out the chimney shaft. It had to be cleaned on the dock with a brush and hose, and I plugged away with a will. "This is a lot easier than cleaning the bilge," I said brightly.

"Oh no," John exclaimed, "look at the state of the dock! There's soot everywhere!"

"Kind of like mud wrestling without the wrestling," I said, digging cheerfully into the chimney. "I can flush it into the ocean when I'm done."

"Oh no you can't," said John. "The soot will stick to the hull of every boat in the marina and none of our neighbours will be speaking to us by tomorrow."

"Oh dear," I said. "How may rolls of paper towel do we own?"

I looked at the dishevelled dock in dismay. A neighbour passed by. "Adding chimney sweep to your list of accomplishments, Catherine?" he asked. "How come John's not covered with soot?"

"I'm supervising," said John. The neighbour chuckled and boarded his boat.

"Do you think he noticed the mess on the dock?" I whispered to John.

"I don't know how he could miss it," said John.

We took a bucket and rag to the dock, flushed it with the hose and then hid inside the boat. "Did anyone besides the one neighbour see us?" I asked. "Who would have thought that stealth, as well as expertise, was necessary to clean a diesel stove?"

"Well," said John, "part of the skill is in not getting caught spraying soot all over the dock. If you can't be tidy, how's your night vision?"

"Not good," I replied. "Besides, surely the neighbours won't mind. Our chimney has been belching soot all winter and our corner of Cowichan Bay looks like an industrial park anyway."

"Everyone knows we have a diesel stove," said John thoughtfully, "but just to be safe, let's pretend we're not home until the next tide. Messy, aren't you?"

I ignored the comment and proceeded to dig into the bowels of the firepot. With my gloved hands, I scooped out an amazing pile of clinkers and placed it carefully on newspaper. I surveyed the result proudly. I dug deeper and came up with a rusted, cone-shaped plug about the length of a nail.

"What is it?" I asked John.

"Haven't a clue," he replied.

"Darling," I explained patiently, "you're the husband. You're supposed to know these things. Should I put it back?"

"Don't know," said John. "Don't know what it's for." I carefully put the plug to one side, ready to add to my collection of odd screws and earrings whose mates had fallen into the bilge.

Next I pulled out the pan under the oven and inserted the nozzle of the vacuum cleaner. With a roar like a bush plane on take off, the vacuum sucked out the bowels of the oven and sprayed soot all over the galley. I turned off the vacuum and stowed it, disposed of my pile of clinkers and turned proudly to John. "Done, darling," I said.

The galley was smeared with soot, the counter tops were black, and there were smudged footprints all over the main saloon. The dock was the colour of pavement and the deck was speckled with soot. My jeans would never be the same again. But the firepot was clean, the chimney was clean, and all the ashes had been sucked out of the holding tray. "Now that I know how to do it," I said, "will I ever have to do it again?"

"You did a fine job," said my husband. "In fact, I think you're practically an expert. You can clean the stove as many times as you like." He grinned. "And more. Let's go up to the pub for a drink."

Provisioning for the Non-Gourmet

"**A** WORLD TRAVELLER such as myself has experience with a broad range of exotic cuisine," said John. "Take the YMCA in Montreal in 1963, for example," he continued. "Every Wednesday night for a dollar fifty I could enjoy the 'YMCA Special' — beans and wieners with a side of toast."

"Darling," I said, "that's not exotic and it's not cuisine. To count as cuisine it has to be edible."

"Scoff all you like," said John. "It was my first introduction to Canadian culture, and I thought it was wonderful."

It was our first trip beyond Cape Keppel, and we were provisioning the boat for an extended voyage of over a week. We hadn't yet decided on a destination — I think John was planning to determine all that depending on the wind direction the Tuesday morning of our departure — but we had decisions to make about food. I leaned toward the "tin can" system of provisioning myself — cereal for breakfast, one can for lunch, three cans for supper and a sack of potatoes. I wish I could lay claim to having invented this system, but I must properly attribute it to the brilliance of a non-cook who had sailed before me. I added one flourish of my own — orange juice to prevent scurvy. Who knew how long our ten day voyage would take? The "Gilligan Island" survivors had only planned on three hours.

It looked like we would be relying heavily on John's culinary favourites. I had tried to walk by the display of pork and beans, but John had stopped the cart and stood gazing with eager interest. "We'll have to stock up," he said. "After all, we'll be gone for ten days. Will ten cans be enough?"

"Mercy — mercy..." I moaned. "Do you remember the time you made yourself pancakes with lemon juice and sugar and you tried to convince me the lemon juice counted as a vegetable? We need vitamins."

"Beans have vitamins," John said. "Beans are a vegetable."

"How about some nice lima beans?" I asked.

"Pooh," said John.

"Look at this beautiful canned corn."

"Ugh," said John.

"My, what lovely sweet potatoes — all cunningly nestled in a tin."

"Don't like them," said John.

"Peas — canned fresh from the farm."

"Yuk," said John.

"Baby carrots — hand-picked for every tin."

"No thanks," said John.

I lost patience." John," I said, "if you pick out ten tins of vegetables, I will be very, very happy. If you don't I will be very, very sad."

"Oh dear," said John, and he threw in ten tins of vegetables he'd picked at random.

The actual eating was a lot less complicated than the provisioning. We ended up stranded at Ganges with coupling problems, and just down the road from the marina, irresistibly calling to us, was a fully-stocked Thrifty's. We dined sumptuously every night on fresh steak and chicken, vegetables with the dew still on them, berries warm from the sun and cream as smooth as liquid velvet. Raspberries and blueberries were in season, and we indulged wildly. After each sumptuous meal, lavish with fresh butter and cold milk, we'd loll around the cabin with extended bellies and sip steaming coffee, congratulating each other on enjoying the use of shore power and hence, our two-burner 110-volt stovetop and our gently-humming freezer. Not for us the rigors of Chunky Soup warmed in a saucepan on a Force Ten barbecue!

Lunches, we spread butter on that day's purchase of fresh bread and added our choice of refrigerated luncheon meat. The crackers and corned beef languished in the provision locker. The orange juice rested quietly in the dark as we sucked back raspberries and swilled ice-cold milk. Breakfasts were real toast, as our toaster was hooked up to shore power, and hot coffee made with a coffee maker. I stowed the aluminum coffee pot with the wire basket in the back of the dry-cereal locker.

The labels started to come loose from the smoked oysters and canned vegetables. I noticed dents in some of the fruit tins. I began to wonder what on earth I'd do with eight canned hams once we returned to Cowichan Bay, and I pondered the probability of John getting sated after ten tins of chicken à la king Chunky Soup. I began to regret leaving my bread maker and crock pot behind. Only real galley experts could crouch over an open flame and turn out a successful meal. The barbecue lay cold and neglected while I indulged myself with electrical appliances, the madness of shore power having seized my brain.

Afternoons we'd stroll to the ice cream parlour and treat ourselves to a cone. Friends invited us out for a breakfast of home-made waffles and raspberry syrup and crisp bacon and Salt Spring coffee, and we ate a lunch of grilled cheese sandwiches and tea in a cabin on an island. I noticed I began to grunt when I bent over, and the washing machines at Ganges shrank all my jeans.

When we finally made it back to Cowichan Bay, all our tinned provisions lay intact, and except for half a sack of potatoes, we were as stocked as when we pulled out.

I took out all the tins of vegetables and lined them up. Then I sighed and put them away. "Beans and wieners tonight, darling," I said, "and toast too, I think. Now that we're back, we'll have to use up all our canned goods, and we may as well start with your favourites."

Ship's Log

CAPTAIN: JOHN DOOK
Crew: Catherine Dook
Vessel: *Inuksuk*

11:00 We are Ganges bound. The engine sounds like poetry. Ten minutes into our voyage, and nothing has gone wrong. There is general rejoicing among the Crew.

11:10 Separation Point. We are safely past.

11:20 Crew breaks out coffee from thermos and congratulates Captain on getting us safely thus far. Engine throbs like a Harley on a hot summer day.

12:00 Cape Keppel. Crew and Captain fondly reminisce about the maiden voyage of the *Inuksuk*, when we melted our engine. Captain requests the Crew stop reminiscing.

12:05 Crew, feeling frisky, asks Captain to race powerboat coming up on port side. Captain ignores request.

12:10 Captain requests chart from below. Crew, realizing that in two years of trying we have never made it past Cape

Keppel, recognizes the gravity of the moment and complies immediately. We are now in new and unknown waters. Crew falls silent.

12:15 Crew asks, "Are we there yet?" Captain responds with dirty look.

12:20 Crew prepares lunch of sandwiches and coffee. Crew decides it would be too difficult to fire up barbecue on stern rail and heat can of soup. Crew pauses to rethink provisioning strategy, which allowed for ten tins of Chunky Soup.

12:30 Isabella Island. Crew suffers momentary panic at not being able to spot lights, then calms down when she realizes it's broad daylight and we still know where we are.

12:45 *Inuksuk* avoids getting run down by ferry at Fulford Harbour. Crew congratulates Captain.

12:45 Crew checks fuel. Registers "full."

13:00 Crew comments that at two hours, this is the longest we have ever run the engine of the *Inuksuk*. Captain responds that to celebrate early is to invite Murphy on board — the invisible crewmember who makes things go wrong. Crew remains cautiously optimistic, though acknowledging the obvious merit of Captain's observation.

13:35 Yeo Point. Crew bursts into a chorus of Conway Twitty's classic, "I Can Tell You've Never Been This Far Before." Captain ignores Crew.

14:00 Crew points out that several landmarks to Ganges Harbour are not marked on chart. Captain discloses that chart is 30 years old. Crew expresses displeasure.

14:30 Crew panics, hollering, "Oh no! Oh no! The chart says only four feet of water here." Captain responds, "That's four metres." "We're going to run aground," yells the Crew. "Nonsense," says the Captain. "This boat draws only six feet." Crew goes below to calm herself and pour another cup of coffee.

14:40 *Inuksuk* approaches Ganges Harbour. Crew begs Captain to drop the hook and take the dinghy in to avoid the trauma of docking. Captain responds that Crew does not know how to drop the hook. Crew counters with information that she is not very good at docking either.

14:45 Captain and Crew successfully dock. Captain and Crew, now speaking to each other again, turn off engine and report to marina. A successful voyage of the *Inuksuk*.

Stranded on Salt Spring

W E WERE AT Salt Spring Marina, and I was perturbed. Here we were, moored at a lovely dock surrounded by million-dollar boats, and nobody seemed to want to look me in the eye. "What's going on?" I asked my husband.

"Well, it may be the way you're dressed," said John.

"Why, what's wrong with the way I'm dressed?" I asked. I was wearing my favourite "fat" jeans with the knees ripped out and a jean shirt from Sears with only one button missing. "This is a coordinated outfit. I'd be the height of fashion at Cowichan Bay," I said.

"Well, it's OK for Cowichan Bay," said John. "There all you're expected to do is hang around the local cafés and look colourful. Here it's different. No offence, but you look like you might ask the tourists for money." I snorted and steadied the bow line. We were just getting ready to cast off, after a wonderful 48 hour stay at Ganges Harbour. We'd visited with old friends, and had a beer at the legendary local pub. We'd walked and explored and shopped to our hearts' content. Now it was time to sail toward the horizon once more — well, maybe toward Pender Island.

John explained the casting-off procedure to me. "I'll untie the stern line and loosen the bow line. When the stern drifts out, release the bow line and I'll reverse us out of here."

"Aye Captain," I replied. "Are you sure you know what you're doing?"

"Of course," John said confidently. "Piece of cake."

"It's a lovely marina," I remarked, "but it costs a fortune and we can't afford to stay much longer."

"Ready!" yelled John, and put the engine in gear. Nothing happened. The wind, blowing briskly down the harbour, flattened us into the dock. I loosened the bow line a little and it dropped into the water. The stern swung sluggishly outward and then collapsed back into the dockside. "Push the stern out," John yelled.

I pulled the bow line on board and ran down the length of the boat with the boathook. Several bystanders saw we were having trouble and ran to help. With everyone pushing, we cleared a small boat, rounded a corner as the bystanders let go, and headed straight for a million-dollar yacht, bow first.

"Reverse! Reverse!" I yelled.

"I can't! Engine's not responding," John hollered back.

I placed both my hands over my eyes and moaned, "Oh my God — we're going to die." The passersby had by this time realized we were in serious trouble — or at least the fibreglass yacht was. Five of them grabbed the bow and heaved. Inch by inch, the *Inuksuk* slowed, and then stopped.

"Heavy boat," commented one of our rescuers, red of face and panting. Tied up, we thanked the men. I staggered off the boat and headed down the dock after them.

"Where are you going?" asked John.

"Dock fees...repair bill...I'm going to ask those tourists for money," I said.

Part II

"SO THE COUPLING gave," said John. "Could have happened to anyone."

"Darling, I love you," I said. "But when you quote Kurt Russell from *Captain Ron*, you make me nervous."

"Well, we're here," John said, "and we have to wait until Monday until we get a repairman. So what do we do?"

I smiled at a passing tourist, who avoided my eyes. "People are so unfriendly here," I commented. "I miss Cowichan Bay and all our friends. When you dock in Cowichan Bay, even if you're a stranger there are always three or four people to pull your boat in and ask personal questions, like 'How come your deck's that rotten colour?' and 'How much did you pay for your boat?' I miss our neighbour coming over with a glass of rum and giving us advice on what modifications we should do with a cement saw. The guy living in the tug calls me 'Mom' and asks what's for dinner. He's so friendly, I'd adopt him in a minute if beer was a tax deduction. My girlfriends are always telling me about the times they forgot their children on shore and they give me great recipes. Our Ganges mechanics took a beer break yesterday." I paused dramatically.

"Can't we get that nice religious marine mechanic from Cowichan Bay?"

"Stop whimpering," said my beloved. "These guys are experts. I'm learning new things from them all the time."

"The bilge is full of unidentified pieces of boat," I said darkly, "and I can't wait to get back to Canada — this marina is positively bristling with American flags."

"They are strangers in a strange land," said John, "and you should be nice to them."

"Salt Spring Island isn't strange," I said, "it's beautiful and quaint. It's Cowichan Bay that's strange, and I miss it."

"What could be more Canadian than taking a beer break?" asked my husband. "In fact, I think I'll have one myself. Lots of Cowichan Bay residents take beer breaks. In fact, I suspect lots of Cowichan Bay residents have beer for breakfast. Can I have beer for breakfast?"

I sniffed my disapproval and settled in for a good sulk.

A crowd of nattily-dressed tourists parted in front of two scruffy-looking men wearing jeans and carrying tools. "Our marine mechanics are coming," said John.

"Are they sober?" I asked snottily.

"Of course," said John. I eyed them with suspicion. The two men looked like Caribbean pirates. I noted with disapproval a pigtail and an ear stud. But they greeted us politely and crawled into the engine room.

"Would you please pass me that wrench?" asked the one with the pigtail. "Thanks, Buddy, oh — and that screwdriver, if you don't mind."

"Of course," said his friend.

"I'd like to back out of here — mind I don't step on you."

I stared at John in astonishment. I hadn't heard such exquisite manners since my last Tupperware party.

I noticed that the pigtail was neat, and the ear stud small and inconspicuous. I warmed to them immediately. "Coffee, anyone?" I asked.

"No, thank you," said the man with the pigtail, "but you folks go ahead — we'll be done by the time you've finished your second cup." The last of my reserve melted and I was completely charmed. I grabbed my husband's arm.

"These guys are terrific," I whispered. "Can we invite them to dinner?"

"You never seem to find a happy medium, do you?" asked my husband. "Chances are they don't want to come to dinner."

I took my coffee on deck to enjoy the sun. An American tourist was on the dock cooking crabs. "Some nice-looking beasts you have there," I ventured. His face lit up with a slow, warm smile.

"They're good crabs," he said. "They'll make a fine feast. Is your boat cement?" We exchanged pleasantries, and I went below with my mug in a thoughtful state of mind.

"You know," I said to my husband, "an American dressed in immaculate whites can be friendly, and tough-looking Canadian mechanics can be mechanical experts and polite enough for any formal drawing room. I think I like the people on Salt Spring Island. They're as strange and wonderful as the folks at Cowichan Bay."

The Shakedown Cruise — or "Whaddya mean that's Sidney? We're supposed to be in Cowichan Bay"

"GOOD HEAVENS," SAID my friend, "It's the height of July and high noon to boot. Why are you wearing that fluorescent orange foul-weather gear?"

"Cute, isn't it?" I asked. "We bought it cheap at Boater's Exchange and I'm trying it on for size. I'm proud to announce I still fit a 'large.' We need it for our trip this summer."

"A cruiser suit in July?" asked my friend.

"I'd hate to be caught unprepared in the first summer typhoon to hit Salt Spring Island," I said. "If it gets dangerous, I'll stand out on the deck in my cruiser suit and wave my arms and yell, 'Here I am, Lord. Save me! Save me!' I'll be easier for God to spot if I'm dressed in orange." There was a pause.

"Do you have an alternate plan?" she asked.

"Well, yes, now that you mention it," I said. "I can always phone someone on my cell phone and ask them to come out to rescue us. This strategy has never failed."

"If you're as far away as Salt Spring, signalling God might have a better chance of success," said my friend.

"I shall draw up a list of phone numbers of people at Cowichan Bay who haven't yet towed us home," I continued.

"Is there anyone left?" asked my friend.

"Lots of people haven't towed us back," I said. "We're trying to get everyone in rotation so we don't wear out our rescue resources." I waved a cheerful goodbye and left.

A week later I was talking to the same friend. "I see you got back early," she said. "How was your holiday?"

"Wonderful," I said. "We started off from Cowichan Bay and motored without any excitement at all to Ganges Harbour. As we were docking, John threw the engine into reverse. The key slipped out of the prop shaft and the prop shaft came out of the coupling."

"No!" gasped my friend. "How awful!"

"Not at all," I said. "We were delirious with delight we hadn't screwed the prop right out of the boat. Besides, we hired two wonderful repairmen who fixed us up in a trice. I've added them to our list of 'Terrific Marine Mechanics I Know.' That very Monday we motored out of Ganges Harbour and headed for Cowichan Bay, waving and signalling to some dear friends who videoed us as we motored past. An hour later, our engine started to miss."

"Oh Glory — not again," said my friend. "What did you do?"

"Well, it wasn't as bad as it sounds. For starters, the prop shaft coupling was sound as a dollar. It held up beautifully. We were very pleased with the job the mechanics at Ganges Harbour had done. There wasn't any wind, so we couldn't sail, and then the engine shut down altogether and the tide started to draw us into the rocks."

"Dreadful!" said my friend. "What happened then?"

"Well, I started to cry with the sheer joy of living. The evening was so beautiful, and the waves were lapping against us so gently as we were being sucked into the rocks, and the man I love was so determined to spend a romantic night with me, he refused to radio for help. After I sobbed for awhile, however, he reluctantly allowed me to phone our neighbours, and a concerned posse of neighbours set out to rescue us, just as the sun was setting."

"Praise heaven," said my friend. "Did they find you?"

"Well, after awhile," I said. "We managed to start the engine again, so we set out to meet them, but we were so delighted that the engine worked, we set out in the wrong direction and by 11:00 PM the lights of Sidney were shining in our eyes and we were surrounded by so many hazard lights I thought it was Christmas." My friend was silent. "Our engine quit completely, and our depth sounder registered fifty feet, but our depth sounder was mistaken, because John let out one hundred and twenty feet of chain with the anchor and it didn't catch and then it jammed so we couldn't pull it up again and there we were — drifting helplessly in the dark with one hundred and twenty feet of chain hanging straight down. The silent moon and the dozens of hazard lights in the velvet dark were the only witnesses to the gentle recriminations I affectionately offered to the man I married. The night was brilliant with emotion. I gave our latitude and longitude from our GPS to our neighbours, and they arrived, just like cavalry, at midnight. It was the high point of the whole holiday, and there had been several moments of excitement up to that time. It took John and two neighbours to fix the anchor and the other boat towed us safely home. At 2:00 AM we quietly slid into our slip. I was overcome with delight and thankfulness and later — rum. It's all clear to me now why sailors drink."

"It sounds like it was quite the holiday," said my friend.

"John says I have enough material now for a disaster movie. The following day John was talking to our marine mechanic and he told him our lives were never in danger. I told him, 'Darling YOUR life was in danger.' But here we are safe and sound and even more remarkable, still married. You know, I didn't even have to wear my cruiser suit. God has guardian angels who can plot a position from GPS coordinates. Who would have thought the Almighty was high tech?"

Stage Two

"**H**OW COME YOU tweaked my nose when you went past?" I asked John. "Time was you used to kiss me instead."

"Oh dear," said my neighbour. "You've been married for nearly three years now — looks like stage two."

"What's stage two?" I asked.

"I don't like to say," she replied ominously. "I'll let you find out naturally."

"I didn't marry her willingly," said John. "The JP said, 'Do you take this woman to be your lawful wedded wife, and do you want a drink,' and I happened to be thirsty."

I turned to my neighbour. "Immediately after the wedding, there was a most undignified wrangling between my new husband and my father. Dad said he was entitled to a bride price, and John said he wanted a dowry. Finally John agreed to send Dad two pregnant goats as soon as I got a job."

"And did he?" asked my neighbour.

"Not yet," I replied.

"Just what I said — stage two," said my neighbour.

"Is it stage two when you get lost and aim for Sidney instead of Cowichan Bay and have to get towed home and when you get home your husband's *National Enquirer* horoscope reads, 'You may not have a clear picture of where you're going,' and you laugh so hard you nearly fall overboard?"

"Sounds like stage two to me," said my neighbour.

"I knew exactly where I was," said John.

"But only after we got there, darling," I said.

"It was all my fault," said John. "I listened to you."

"I may have been a little confused," I admitted. "Southeast looks nearly like southwest on the compass, especially in the dark. It was a mistake anybody could make. Besides, Sidney is a lovely city. I would have enjoyed visiting it. But the search and rescue team insisted we go home with them. Really! They seemed to imply it wasn't safe for us to be drifting around in the dark. I guess they were right. It wasn't safe for you, darling. I told you not to listen to me when I'm wrong."

"Stay calm, Catherine," said John. "As I recall, your horoscope read, 'Keep your temper and feelings under control the 28th.' You didn't follow that excellent advice. You burst into sobs and hollered, 'I want our neighbour! I want Fred. Fred knows what he's doing and you obviously don't.' My feelings were hurt."

"Stage two," said my neighbour.

"Are you in stage two, as well?" I asked.

"I'll say," she replied. "The other day my husband said that if I died he wouldn't have the heart to keep the boat — he'd sell it 'What?' I yelled, 'twenty years living on board a boat with you and some OTHER woman gets a HOUSE?' I hardly spoke to him for a week."

"Is it stage two," I asked her, "when your husband sets you

problems multiplying pounds, shillings and pence by seven instead of spending the evening telling you how beautiful you are and how lucky he is?"

"I'd be luckier if I had a wife who could multiply," said John. "How are we supposed to go offshore if you can't do the simple calculations involved in celestial navigation?"

"How are we supposed to get home from Ganges if you listen to me every time I give an incorrect reading from the compass?" I asked.

"Stage two for sure," said my neighbour. "Maybe even stage three."

"And furthermore," I said, "how do the intricacies of the British currency system of thirty years ago relate to celestial navigation?"

"It's all part of my plan," said John.

"Is this the same plan that jammed the anchor the night we got lost?" I asked.

"A minor miscalculation," said my husband. "A wife in stage one would have forgotten all about it by now."

"I bet you've forgotten all about the coffee I made for you on the barbecue when we were being towed home," I said.

"No, my dear. It was a little cool, but it was the most delicious instant coffee I've ever tasted," he said. "It was sort of like drinking one of those exotic chilled coffees."

"The moon was full. It was a lovely night," I said. "The sky was full of stars and it was warm. In different circumstances I'd have called it romantic."

"That's true," said John.

"And that docking you did in the pitch dark with a crippled motor was a beautiful job," I said.

"Thank you, Catherine," said John.

"You've regressed all the way back to stage one," said my neighbour. "I think I'm going home now."

I picked up the *National Enquirer*. "My horoscope says, 'Exciting changes are ahead.' Does this mean we'll fix the engine?" I sighed.

"Of course," said John. "Remember — every voyage with me is an adventure." And he kissed me.

"Only a woman in stage one would go with you, darling," I said, and I kissed him back.

Celestial Navigation — or "Where are we?"

"**I**F WE'RE GOING offshore," I told John, "I'm not going to bet my life on a GPS. I plan to learn celestial navigation. Besides, my girlfriends all tell me men never ask for directions."

"Go right ahead," said John. "One of us should know how to use a sextant."

My husband's approval spurred me on to actual activity. I bought four books on celestial navigation and took the plastic sextant out of its case. As I held it firmly in my hands, I could feel the mystery fall away like shedding water. I pushed and pulled the little sliding thingamy and looked through the eyepiece. "You're holding it upside down," said my husband. I put the sextant back in its case and turned to the first page of the first book.

Hours later, I was convinced of five indisputable truths.

1. The earth rotates around the sun.
2. The Pacific is a large ocean chock full of latitude and longitude.
3. The stories you hear about people learning navigation as they go with a twelve dollar plastic sextant and a four page instruction booklet are greatly exaggerated.

4. I should have studied trigonometry in high school.
5. Cowichan Bay doesn't have a horizon.

Undaunted, I turned to a book entitled, *Navigation for the Complete Idiot*. The title filled my breast with hope. Wasn't I perimenopausal and suffering from large lapses in my short term memory? I was the most qualified person I knew. The thought cheered me immensely, and I sat down again to read.

Much later, I had added considerably to my knowledge of navigation. In theory I was fully capable of finding longitude, with the minor drawback that:

1. I still couldn't use a sextant, and
2. I didn't know how to use the tables.

"I have an idea," I said to my husband. "How do you feel about sailing up and down meridians of longitude? According to my map the West Coast runs nearly due north and south. We could sail up and down the West Coast, relying on the signs in ports to tell us which community we're in and then look up the latitude on our map. For example, the Cowichan Bay Harbour Authority sign is a pretty strong indication we're in Cowichan Bay. We'll never be lost using this system as long as we stick to meridians of longitude and we can interpret signs written in Spanish as we sail south."

"Not a very workable idea," said John. "You'll have to understand both navigation and Spanish, and unfortunately you have a firm grasp of neither. I think it's back to the books. Besides," he continued, "the plan is we sail to Hawaii and that'll require latitude as well as longitude."

One memorable voyage the very following summer we got lost between Ganges and Cowichan Bay — a feat not equalled by many navigators — and I determined we needed even more help than the "Idiot" book could give us. We signed up for a course on celestial navigation — a bring-your-own-sextant-and-learn-it-all-in-one-day extravaganza that left us reeling. The instructor was personable and a whiz. We started slow. "There are no stupid questions," he asserted confidently.

"Which is latitude and which is longitude? My mind's a blank," I said, and I saw him flinch every so slightly.

As the day progressed and our instructor warmed to his subject, he stepped up the pace. Calculations for determining longitude flashed by us with effortless speed. We sat riveted to our chairs, incomprehension swirling in the room thick as methane gas on beans-on-toast night. He explained the determination of latitude by sun shot in four minutes with the skilled precision of a skipper docking a power vessel with side-thrusters in calm water at midday, and though we were left gasping at the beauty and accuracy of the feat, I didn't feel I could duplicate it with the same graceful speed.

We trudged home thoughtfully, carrying our sextant. "I learned a lot," I said enthusiastically. "I think I can handle dead reckoning and longitude both. Can we get to Hawaii using dead reckoning and longitude? Can I practice getting us to Ganges next summer?"

My husband is a wise man — the kind of guy who can tell at a glance the difference between Sidney and Cowichan Bay, even at night. "No, Catherine," he said, "I let you navigate last summer, and look where it got us...next summer, we shall practice using the instruments we have. Let's start by turning on the GPS..."

Too Many Children

"DARLING, I LOVE you," I said, "but we have too many children."

"This is all your fault," said my husband. "I keep getting rid of them and you keep on inviting them back."

The *Inuksuk* was overcrowded. We had my husband and me in the aft cabin, our six foot handicapped son Paul in the forward cabin, son John Jr. in the main saloon and son Rupert living in a float home nearby and dropping by for meals. "It's your sons," I complained. "They wash too much. They shower at the drop of a hat, and we're pumping out grey water faster than we can pump in fresh. It's not natural to be so clean. Now take me and Paul for example — I wouldn't go so far as to call us slobs, but..."

"I would," said John, "and Paul eats more groceries than the Canadian Armed Forces."

"There's more numbers on your side of the family," I said, "so it all evens out. Besides, I'm the one cooking for five without an oven. If it wasn't for my crock pot I'd have to roast whole pigs over a campfire on the dock." I paused for breath. "Our grocery bill is adding up like the national debt, and if we didn't eat groceries at the rate we do, we'd sink the boat on shopping days. As it is, I can barely get them put away before they're eaten. It's lucky the boys are not fussy eaters, even if they do prefer your beans and eggs and chips to my meat and potatoes. But what I really object to are the lineups at the head. Some morning I'm going to have to pee right into the bilge, and then you'll be sorry."

"I certainly will," said John. "Everyone knows a crew worth its salt pees over the side of the boat."

"We have neighbours with a delicate sense of propriety," I retorted in my most dignified manner. "Let's negotiate a way to schedule head time instead." There was a pause.

"All right," said John. "In the interest of freeing up the head, I'll forego my spring wash."

"Such sacrifice, darling," I sighed, "and speaking of washing, there's a sack full of laundry crying out to be carted up to the Bluenose Marina and put through the machines. See if you can hit up some of our children for quarters."

"I can't ask our sons for money," said John. "Rupert changed over all our fuel valves to make them more accessible and solved all our electrical problems with one go at the breaker panel. John helped build the deck head, and Paul laughs at my jokes."

"That's true," I said, "and I think it's wonderful all three of you will watch 'Teletubbies' just to keep Paul happy. It's lucky you're not too particular about what programs you watch."

"Do we have a choice?" asked John.

"Frankly, no, darling," I said, "but it's nice of you all the same. And there are some real advantages to having all our sons on board. They're remarkably handy to have around when we're sailing. Rupert can fix anything, John can leap from a moving boat onto a heaving dock carrying a mooring line without falling into the ocean, and Paul sits still in the cockpit. They're a fine group, and I think we should keep them all. They eat anything we cook and appreciate it, and at night the boat is filled with happy sounds and the roar of the electric head."

"You're right, Catherine. They are a good bunch."

"Good night, John."

"Good night, Catherine."

"Good night, Rupert."

"Good night, Catherine."

"Good night, John Jr."

"Good night, Catherine."

"Good night, Paul."

"Mum!"

"Okay now — everybody shut up and go to sleep."

"Good night, Dad."

"I mean it!"

"Oh, darling?"

"Hmmmmm?"

"I forgot to mention — daughter Maggie phoned today. She's sending the three grandkids for a visit next week. I told her we'd be delighted. Sweet dreams, darling."

Technical Terms

IT'S THE CRACK of dawn — or at least 9:00 AM sharp. Through clouds of cigarette smoke at the local restaurant, one can dimly see the workings of a cultural phenomenon — sociological groups of immense interest — the gathering of the locals for morning coffee. Half-conscious men in rumpled clothing, some in baseball caps, grimly drag themselves to small tables in clearly marked groupings, determined to fulfill the social obligations requisite to a resident of Cowichan Bay. They sit collapsed and unspeaking, except to call aloud for hot beverages in varying tones of anguish.

Soon a genial exchange of pleasantries and information begins.

"For two years I've had morning coffee with John and John and Jim and Bob," I tell John, "and I've never understood a word."

One major theme of their conversation appears to have been where they can get bottom paint that works. If someone would find a way to mix agent orange into bottom paint, there would be a market for it at Cowichan Bay. All you have to say is, "I mixed it myself," and there is a respectful pause in the conversation. Of course, everyone knows bottom paint is effective for only twelve months no matter what's in it — pickling spices, peppercorns, cayenne pepper or black jellybeans. At least I think that's what they said.

And then there was the time John (not my husband — the other one) was talking about replacing the gas engine in his sailboat.

"What you need is a little one-lunger," said Jim, leaning forward to tap his cigarette into an ashtray.

"My Glory," I gasped, "a short marine mechanic with cancer?" Four unsmiling faces turned in my direction. There was an awkward pause.

"A one-lunger," said Jim, carefully enunciating each word, "is a one-cylinder diesel engine." The men avoided looking at each other.

"Oh," I said, and I tried to look nonchalant as I sipped my coffee. I was too embarrassed to ask what a cylinder was.

John (not my husband — the other one) described towing his little sailboat into its new slip. "I thought it had an engine," I said innocently.

"Of course," said John patiently, "but I'm taking it out."

"Didn't you take out the engine in your last boat?" I asked. My husband kicked me under the table. John ignored me.

"The wind was blowing like crazy, and Bob was rowing like a madman."

"Wind blows predominantly in the wrong direction," Jim commented.

"You have to fool it," said John.

"The Spanish Armada took thirteen days to sail one hundred and fifty miles — they arrived starving," said my husband. At last they were talking about something I could relate to!

72

"It was the English diet that sent them screaming back to Spain," I remarked.

"Murphy was in his glory," said John, doggedly turning the conversation back to things nautical.

"Are you going to buy that little diesel engine from the States?" asked Jim.

"I think so," said John. "Of course, I'll have to take it through customs."

"Use a mock up of the engine with con-rods sticking out," said Bob. The men chuckled.

"What's a con-rod and why isn't it supposed to stick out?" I asked, unable to contain myself.

"A con-rod is a rod that connects the piston to the crank-shaft," said my husband patiently. "Con-rods up and down — good. Con-rods sticking out unconnected to pistons or crank-shaft — bad." He looked pleased with himself. "Enough definitions. Drink up your coffee, Catherine — we're leaving to run errands." We paid the waitress and left the restaurant.

"What's a cylinder?" I asked, "and do they come in an assortment of colours? Would you like one for Christmas?"

"No more questions," said my husband, "or people will think I'm hired to take you out for walks."

Communication between the sexes is a pattern of parallels, but morning coffee in the local restaurant will someday cross those barriers. Perhaps in a hundred years.

Letters Home

Dear Mom:

So far, we love living aboard. We've just fired up the oven for the winter and, knock wood, it seems to be purring along just fine. Of course, there's a slight diesel odour, but I'm sure we'll get used to that. I've noticed the head is a little cool in the mornings, but the climate is quite mild here so it's not a hardship. All is well here.

Love, Catherine

PS — It's raining today.

Dear Mom:

I've noticed that the odour of diesel permeates everything. My co-workers have started to shun me. Possibly it's because I've also stopped taking showers — it's so cold in the head my wet feet stick to the floor. Tonight we noticed a slight drip in the main saloon, but I imagine most boats drip at least a little. All is well here.

Love, Catherine

PS — It's still raining.

Dear Mom:

I think I may be allergic to diesel. We have some hard choices ahead of us — a warm and cozy boat and possible anaphylactic shock, or death by hypothermia. No biggie — I'm sure we'll cope. Tonight we were watching TV in the main saloon when a big drip fell on the TV, blowing it up and plunging the cabin into darkness. All is well here.

Love, Catherine

PS — It rained again today.

Dear Mom:

I was fired this week. The boss cited "inattention to personal hygiene" and "offensive body odour." It's a pity I lost my job, because the TV is going to cost two hundred dollars to fix. The head is still cold, but I shall have to take showers again if I expect to go on a job search. Wish me luck. All is well here.

Love, Catherine

PS — It's raining.

Dear Mom:

I have chilblains all over my body — probably from showering in primitive conditions with cold water. They had the right idea in the Middle Ages — wash only upon birth and after death, which may come upon me prematurely when I catch pneumonia and perish, but no problem — they say it's a painless death. Much better than drowning, which is also a possibility if we don't staunch our drip problem. All is well here.

Love, Catherine

PS — It has been raining for three months.

Dear Mom:

The welfare worker was really mean to me, even after I fished her out of the ocean. I saved her life and she wasn't even grateful. She said the slipping gangplank was my fault and then she wouldn't give us any money to fix the TV. But she said offensive body odour was an inadequate reason for firing me and she's prepared to plead with my former employer on my behalf. "Just so long," she said, "as I don't have to make another visit." All is well here.

Love, Catherine

PS — It rained today.

Dear Mom:

I got my job back, we turned off the diesel oven and now that it's stopped raining the boat doesn't drip anymore. Even the head is warm. We went for a sail today. Living on a boat is the most fun I've ever had. All is well here.

Love, Catherine

PS — I've noticed the bilge pumps seem to be going off a lot.

(Dear Readers: This was a joke -- I was never fired, I didn't have a welfare worker and really, it *doesn't* rain that much here, does it?)

The Haul-Out

I T WAS FOUR years ago that I'd uttered these prophetic words: "Darling," I'd said, "girlfriends don't paint boats. Fiancées don't paint boats. Wives paint boats. You make me a really good offer like marriage, and we'll talk roller brushes."

"Naturally," John said much later, "I married you as fast as I could. What man wouldn't jump at the chance to have someone paint his boat?" We were sitting in the main saloon, sipping coffee. The *Inuksuk* was docked securely in her slip in Cowichan Bay, where she'd been for the winter season. John drank some coffee and put his mug down with a sigh. "We haven't done the bottom for two years, except to change zincs. I bet we're fastened to the sea floor with mussels." He said the words with a relish and when his eyes fell on me there was a speculative gleam in them that made me suspicious.

"So?" I said casually. I'd avoided the first two haul-outs because my handicapped son had been visiting, and I'd skipped out to the nearest motel with a light heart.

"So it's pay back time," John said, "for making me eat vegetables and criticizing my driving."

"A few tiny words of correction," I said resignedly, "and I'm up to my shins in seafood?"

"It's the fate of every good boat wife to scrape the hull," he said, "and after two years, the seafood will be well past your shins. Got hip waders?"

I changed tack. "It's going to be an awfully heavy job. Are you sure you want to do this?"

John smirked. "I won't be doing it — you will," he said, and finished off his coffee. "Early to bed," he said, "3:00 AM comes early."

I yawned. "Why? What happens at 3:00 AM?"

"High tide," said my beloved, "and somebody has to get the boat on the ways."

I snapped awake.

"You mean it's not all part of the service?"

"Here's how it works," said John. "We'll have help, but we get the boat on the ways. First thing in the morning we scrape the bottom. Then we paint. Then we pay the marine mechanic lots and lots of money."

"And what does the marine mechanic do?" I asked.

"He sells us the paint, rents us the power washer and performs the miracle of the loaves and fishes upon our propeller. Remember the day it became a 1/3 off special when one of the blades snapped off? Well, he is going to expertly install the new one for which we bartered away any hope of a new car. Be nice to him. No spending sprees in Ganges with 2/3 of a propeller."

Three AM did come early — so early that it was almost before I'd gone to sleep when I was awakened by the throbbing motor of the dinghy that was to tow us into position. I threw on some clothes and scrambled up on deck, tripping over two lines and a winch. The dinghy towed us gently across the quiet surface of the inky water while I stood rigidly on the deck clutching our last pike pole. The other one had come to an untimely end in Ganges Harbour the summer before when I had trapped it between a piling and the hard dodger. Having snapped one pike pole dramatically in half, I considered myself practically an expert on pike poles. I stared aggressively at a passing piling, twelve feet out of range on the starboard side. We neared the ways and leaned the *Inuksuk* into position. Following directions, I stepped off the deck and onto the catwalk, clutching a stanchion close to my chest. It occurred to me that if our sixty thousand pound ferrocement boat seriously wanted to list in the opposite direction, chances were that I would not be able to hold it. The thought made my palms slippery, and the stanchion slipped a trifle. Then it dropped a little more. "The boat's moving," I gasped. A reassuring voice came at my ear.

"We're moving up on the ways. The boat is settling on the bottom."

"Oh," I said.

Once high dry and tilted, there was nothing left to do but clamber back into bed, feet aimed downward. John drew me to one side. "You see this bucket?" he said.

"What's it for?" I asked.

"It's instead of the head," he said. "You married me for bucket or for worse."

"I'm not even going to ask what could be worse than a bucket," I said.

"You'll find out tomorrow, my little Snoggy Lips," said the man I married, "because you're first at the power washer."

"You're enjoying this altogether too much," I said.

Morning dawned clear and bright. I climbed gingerly down the catwalk and stood in silence before our 44-foot hull. I turned to John. "If we'd donated these mussels to Molly

Malone, she'd be rich and retired instead of dead and people singing songs about her in pubs. These are the healthiest looking mussels I've ever seen."

We scraped for hours. The power washer roared, the water streamed and a crunchy heap of mussels grew steadily underfoot. There was slime on my hands, gunge on my jeans, fishy-smelling stringy muck in my hair and smudges on my face. Behind me stood a small knot of local men, who had peculiar expressions on their faces. Approving — that was it! As if the sight of a woman up to her knees in bottom gunge and valiantly fighting the good fight with a power washer was an attractive one. John leaned towards my ear. "They're all jealous of me," he said.

"The last time a man at Cowichan Bay looked at me like that I was shovelling snow," I said. "The things you learn about men when you're forty! The magazines tell you you need the egg diet and a push-up bra, but what it really takes is a power washer and a pair of sea boots."

At last the hull was scraped and power washed. Our neighbour, who had scraped yards of hull alongside John and me, lit up a cigarette and leaned against the catwalk. "Should be ready to paint soon," he said. "Lucky it's not raining." I scanned the sky eagerly, looking for clouds.

"If it rains, do we quit for the day?"

"No such luck, my little dumpling," said John. "If it rains, we paint in the rain." He handed me a roller brush. "Hold onto this and familiarize yourself with it while I buy the bottom paint." He hurried off. I sat on the ways and looked at the roller brush. Here we were — me and my roller brush. Destiny had swung me up on a ways with a husband and a roller brush.

Husband, roller brush. I looked at the expanses of denuded hull that had to be painted, and then at John, returning with the paint. Was it worth it? Of course it was. I had a comfortable home to live in, a bucket of my very own and a man who referred to me as "Snoggy Lips." I wished I'd met John twenty years earlier. Then I dipped my roller in the paint.

On the Ways

THE BOAT WAS high in the air, leaned slightly to port and slanted downhill. As I cautiously made my way up the ladder of the ways, I wondered if my weight in the head would tip the *Inuksuk* to starboard and send us all crashing…Nonsense! The *Inuksuk* weighs sixty thousand pounds. I switched my attention to the ways. The ladder looked rickety. I took a step, and the apparatus swayed slightly. The *Inuksuk* weighs sixty thousand pounds. Would the ways support that slight list to port? Or would it give way and send us all crashing…I took another step. The boat was blocked on the starboard side. Would the blocks hold? I considered glancing at them to reassure myself, but I was too frightened of the height I'd attained to look down. I crept insecurely along the two loose planks at the top of the ways parallel to the boat, with my purse strap clutched in my teeth. Torn between my natural inclination to scream out loud and my desire to retain a grip on my purse, I snorted fiercely through my nose, collapsed on my hands and knees on the deck and crawled slowly towards the companionway entrance. I draped my torso over the entrance and with my head poked into the main saloon, I called to my husband in dulcet tones. "My love?" My purse fell from my mouth, landed with a thud on the floor and slid aft. "Did I ever tell you I'm afraid of heights?"

"No," said John, "you never did. Why?" There was a pause. I lay draped over the entranceway, hind end uppermost.

"Well, I thought I might mention it now," I said. "I was wondering if you would be so kind as to assist me in sliding down the ladder? I'm too frightened to stand up."

"Don't be ridiculous," said John.

"Lower your voice, please," I begged. "The sound vibrations might tip us over." John reached up and half-dragged, half-lifted me into the main saloon. I landed with a thud and lay in a heap on the floor, quaking with fear. "We're going over," I moaned. I slid slightly aft. "We're going in." I clutched John by the knees.

"For heaven's sake!" John exclaimed. "We're on dry land in a sixty thousand pound ferrocement boat. We're not going anywhere."

"Sixty thousand pounds!" I moaned. "How strong is that cable?"

"I swear to you," said John solemnly, "that we will not fall starboard, we will not fall port, and we will not slide into the water."

"Unless the cable snaps," I said, sitting up on the floor.

"The cable is not going to snap," said John, assisting me onto a settee berth.

"How do you know?" I asked.

"I'm the husband. I know these things," said John soothingly.

"John," I said.

"Yes?" he said.

"Let's not go out tonight."

"Whatever you want, my little dumpling," said John.

83

"John," I said.

"Yes?" he said.

"Would you mind sitting over there, across from me, to balance the boat?"

"Of course," said John.

"John?" I said.

"Yes?" he said.

"It's going to be a long night, isn't it?"

"I always agree with you," said John.

Part III

FIRST EVENING ON the ways, and all was quiet. John and I sat in the main saloon and looked at each other. I shifted myself slightly. "I'm getting used to the slant," I said brightly. There was a pause.

"There's no TV," said John. He looked around the saloon. "What'll we do all evening?"

"We've already tried out the bucket," I said, "so that avenue of amusement is closed to us for awhile." There was another pause.

"Cup of coffee?"

"We're running on one breaker," said John. "This afternoon when I ran the microwave, I blew the breaker and now our marine mechanic has locked up and gone home so I can't get to the breaker and we don't have any power. Sorry." We looked at each other again. "We could go to Snuffy's for fish and chips," said John.

"We can't afford to eat out," I said repressively. "Why don't we talk to each other?"

"We're married," said John. "What have we got to talk about?"

"Lots of married people talk to each other," I said. "Just free associate and say whatever comes into your head."

"Okay," said John. He thought for a minute. "I'm ready," he said. "Are you ready to hear it?"

"Sure," I said.

"You're sure?" said John.

"Of course," I said. "Go ahead."

"I would make a great exotic dancer," said John. "I could use knee pads as my gimmick. I bet women would love to stuff five dollar bills in my knee pads."

"Of course they would, darling," I said comfortingly, "but surely you can think of a more dignified way to spend your golden years."

"I'm already invested with a mantle of dignity," said John. "When I was about to marry Louise many years ago, the Inuit village elders told her she was going to marry a white god, and gave her advice on how to act. I think you should take me to Sunday school for show and tell."

"Thanks for the offer, darling," I said, "but I must decline on a point of theology — no offense." There was another pause.

"I watched an interesting program on TV yesterday," John said. "On earwax. Did you know that a Q-tip is exactly the same size as your ear canal and when you dig around your ear with one you're actually pushing your earwax to the centre of your head?"

"I can't say I've ever given it much thought," I said consideringly. "In fact, I think I can safely say I've never thought about it at all."

"That's because you don't watch TV," said John. "You're missing out on one of life's great educational experiences."

"Like 'Sharpe's Rifles' and the Space Channel?"

"Exactly my point," said John. There was another pause. "I wonder what the world smells like to a dog," John said thoughtfully.

I leaped to my feet slightly rocking the boat. "Enough conversation, darling," I said. "You win. Let's go to Snuffy's for fish
and chips."

John grinned.

"But just promise me one thing, darling," I said. "No knee
pads or free associating in public."

I walked gingerly down the middle of the boat, bent against
the slant. As I reached the ladder, John said, "Pity — I bet they'd
love my knee pads at Snuffy's…"

It's Never Too Late!

WHEN I FIRST announced to my family that I was going to marry John and live on a boat, the pronouncement created a great many comments — most of them expressions of surprise that I'd actually landed a husband. The general feeling among family members had been that the bottom had fallen out of the market. My brothers-in-law, who had visions of supporting me in my old age, were particularly enthusiastic at the thought of my impending nuptials, and were prepared to welcome John into the family with all expressions of camaraderie and goodwill. My parents' relief expressed itself in a lavish reception for the entire Dook extended family, and when I told my mother that John and I planned to go offshore together, she said, "Well dear, have a good time." My father hoped aloud that marriage would give me something to do besides write the humorous book about my childhood I'd threatened to publish.

But one of my sisters was more reluctant about my marriage, and expressed some reservations.

"A boat!" she said. "Really, Catherine doesn't know anything about boats."

"Catherine doesn't know anything about men either," said my brother-in-law cheerfully, "but I'm sure she'll learn. Besides, look at it this way. How much housework is there to do on board a boat?"

"You're absolutely right, dear," said my sister. "Hardly any at all. It'll be perfect for her."

Well, it is perfect for me. But my sister was wrong about one thing. It takes a lot to keep a boat clean and tidy. My husband is at it constantly.

If you don't stow it, it's strewn. We have a "miscellaneous" drawer full of scissors and thread and needles and batteries that we might use some day, screws, bits of hardware, and tools that would get lost in the toolbox. We also have a copy of the lyrics to Ted Wesley's "Bush Plane" typed on notepaper 20 years earlier with a portable manual typewriter, an old address book and two lighters. When we go into a frenzy of tidying on a Saturday afternoon, "small stuff" gets put into that locker.

"Medium-sized stuff" is stuffed into a cubbyhole alongside the navigation table. Because it's an open locker, my husband insists that the objects in it have to meet two criteria: they have to be vaguely nautical, and they have to fit. Videos, for example, are not allowed. It's full of radios and a camera, binoculars and a wind meter.

The bookcases positively bristle with volumes on weather signs and offshore tips, at least on the starboard side of the *Inuksuk*. The port side boasts my less nautical library, which includes Charles Dickens novels, a biography of Henry VIII, Gail Sheehy on negotiating the change of life with grace and élan, and Mrs. Beeton's cookery book — all of them, I argue to my husband, necessary on board a boat.

Every now and then, when clutter gets the best of us, you will find my knitting, a textbook on nursing I found at a thrift store, and past issues of *The Boat Journal* piled up on one end of the settee berth. On top of them is a tangle of bills, paid and unpaid, mail I haven't yet sorted and cassette tapes of Susan Aglukark's Christmas music and Bob Seeger's hits.

"Big stuff" gets heaved into the forward cabin — that computer that's too big to fit into the main saloon, the sewing machine I want to put into storage, unwashed laundry in a plastic garbage bag and the coat that was too wet to put into the hanging locker yesterday.

My husband and I are very clean and tidy people. The only differences are in the rhythm of our cleaning cycles. John blitzes the boat once a day. I feel the urge to clean once a month or so — and then only if it's necessary.

Yes, when the full moon gleams on the water, I can be found with my head buried in the locker by the galley, flinging out hundreds of unused plastic grocery bags (bought from Superstore for four cents each), to get to the cleaning and polishing supplies stored at the bottom of the locker. I smack my lips and forage for cleaning cloths. "Aha," I say gloatingly, "Comet, teak oil, J-cloths, one set of knee pads, rubber gloves, bucket, Mr. Clean, bleach, vinegar, baking soda, scrub brush..." The pile grows in a scattered heap around my knees.

There is a plaintive voice from behind me. "When's supper?"

"Don't be ridiculous, darling," I say, running hot water into the bucket and strapping on the knee pads. "I think I'll start with the head and work aft. If you help me pull up the floor, maybe I can tackle the bilges under the main saloon."

"But I'm hungry," says John.

"I wonder if it's sunny enough to rinse out these settee cushions and lay them out. You don't mind sitting on bare boards for a day or two, do you, John?"

"I wouldn't mind some food," he says. "Do you have any money?"

"Money? No, not on me, darling," I say, piling settee cushions busily in one corner. "Mind you don't knock over my bucket."

"Maybe Marilyn will let me have an order of fries on credit at Snuffy's," John says pathetically. "If she's not too busy. They're usually pretty busy at suppertime."

I'm proud to say my brother-in-law's faith in me was completely justified. Not only have I nearly become a passable housekeeper, but I have become expert at detecting the subtle nuances of meaning behind every utterance of the man I love.

You're never too old to learn.

Safe at Anchor

THE BOAT BOBBED once, and I heard a seagull squawk overhead. A shaft of sunlight streamed in through the porthole and illuminated the bewhiskered face of the man lying next to me. "Wake up, handsome stranger. Do we know each other?" I asked.

"Very funny," said my husband. "I'm first at the head." I yawned and stretched myself, wiggling my toes. A glance out the porthole confirmed that we hadn't dragged the anchor, and I was correspondingly cheerful as I clambered out of the aft berth.

Absolutely nothing had gone wrong the day before. The engine didn't baulk, we didn't hit another boat and we didn't get lost. We didn't run out of fuel, we didn't melt the engine and we didn't lose the dinghy. Not once did I scream from the bow, "Reverse! Reverse! We're going to hit that boat!" nor did I snap any pike poles in half, drop the anchor overboard or foul the prop with the dinghy line.

"You look pleased with yourself," John said as he entered the main saloon.

"I'm getting good at this sailing thing," I said. "Do you know what happened yesterday, darling? Nothing, that's what. Not one teensy marine disaster."

"We didn't go anywhere yesterday," John said. "We were at anchor all day here at Portland Island."

"I know," I sighed with happiness. "Wasn't it lovely? I sat in the cockpit in the streaming sun and read sweaty sea-adventures filled with streaking sea-foam, mainsails in shreds, masts snapping like matchsticks and terrified crew huddled below amid shards of flying glass. Every time a passing ferry wake hit us I nearly had a heart attack. I may not be much of a sailor, but I have 'fear' down pat. I can hardly wait until we go off-shore and I can put all I've learned into practice. The panic when we lose sight of land, the terror at heavy seas and the discomfort at high winds. Don't you love the word 'discomfort?' They use it during childbirth at about seven centimetres dilation. 'Are you in any discomfort?' they ask in little chirpy voices. So I think the word is precisely correct to describe a reaction to typhoon-class winds."

"We're low on coffee," John remarked, ignoring me.

"Low on coffee?" I gasped. "We have to go back! What happens if we run out?"

"My little dumpling," John said, "you are exciting yourself with too much stimulating literature. You should stick to Jane Austen where nothing ever happens."

"I wouldn't call Darcy's cutting remarks about Elizabeth Bennett nothing," I said. "But I see your point. I may be inflaming myself needlessly. I think I'll go for a quiet row after breakfast."

"Shore leave is cancelled for today," John said. "We weigh anchor after breakfast."

I scrambled eggs and perked coffee on the propane camp stove on the deck in the luxurious morning sunshine. I was delighted to notice that the propane hadn't leaked or exploded. The coffee didn't boil over, the eggs didn't burn and when a ferry passed us and the boat rocked to port, I deftly snatched the coffee pot from the stove and held it aloft as the boat rocked wildly underneath my feet. The propane camp stove did not pitch into the sea, nor did the eggs slide off the burner. When I washed up, the water pressure pump cut in and out quickly, indicating that the tank was nearly full.

"Darling," I said, "once in my youth when I'd fouled up the typing of an invoice, an accountant gave me advice so wise I've tried to live my life by it. He said, 'Only people who don't do anything don't make mistakes.'"

I paused for effect. "The moral is obvious. Don't do anything, and you won't make any mistakes. Let's stay here for another day and drink tea and listen to the distress calls on channel 16. Let's put off being one of the boats the Coast Guard has to rescue for one more day — there's a darling."

"Mutiny," said John weakly. But I could tell my argument was persuasive.

"Who knows what perils await us between here and Bedwell Harbour?" I asked. "Why go adventuring on the high seas, tempting fate and our engine with an untried and frightened crew when we're anchored in Paradise? With a stern line fastened to the shore for extra security, I might add. I can spend the day relaxing on the deck reading improving literature. I promise I'll read about something besides sea disasters and we can weigh anchor and hoist our sails tomorrow."

"Oh, all right," John said.

"Darling," I said, flinging my arms around his neck.

"Let go — we're married," John said.

"Sailors always get affectionate in port," I said.

"But they don't usually kiss each other," John said. "Go read a book."

"Whatever you say, Captain," I said. I clambered up the companionway balancing a cup of coffee and a novel.

"What's your choice of reading material for today?" John asked. "Nothing too stimulating, I hope."

I sighed and settled myself in the cockpit. "Oh, it's not nautical at all, darling," I said. "It's called *The Inner Bitch*. I should be fearless by lunchtime."

"Oh no!" John exclaimed. "This is what comes of educating the lower classes." He hurried to port and lowered himself into the dinghy.

"Where are you going, handsome stranger?" I asked.

"I'm going in search of provisions," he said, casting off and starting to row. "Maybe someone on one of those other boats has a copy of *Emma*. I'll tell them it's a marine emergency."

Boarded!

I T WAS LATE at night. I flipped on a twelve-volt light in the galley and opened the door to the locker. I reached inside. Past my fingers flashed an insect — sleek, dark and moving fast. I slammed the door shut and snapped into "alert" mode. With trembling legs I walked three steps into the main saloon. By the time I got to the settee berth, my emotional state had mutated from alert to panic to hysteria. I grabbed my husband by both shoulders. "John! John!" I sobbed, "We've been boarded by roaches." Then I collapsed on his chest in a paroxysm of grief and rage and fear.

"Oh, is that all?" said John, patting my shoulder kindly. "Well, most boats sailing the tropics get roaches. It's ten o'clock. I wonder what's on the Space Channel." I sat up.

"Darling," I said, "I don't think you understand. One roach sighting represents a hundred and fifty other roaches — all of them sexually active. And we're not in the tropics. We're in Cowichan Bay in what was once a roach-free environment. I used to be so happy," I continued, sniffling quietly into my hankie. "I never asked for much out of life — earrings for my birthday, a little sock yarn, a working head…and now my happiness is gone. Gone, gone, gone…"

"They're just bugs," said John weakly. I grabbed his arm.

"They're bugs that will be with us until we die or burn the boat," I cried. "They're bugs that are small and fast and mean and will brand us forever the social pariahs of the dock. At pot luck dock parties people will edge away from my Tuna Noodle Surprise, and visitors will drink their coffee on the deck, even in the rain. Nobody will come boating with us and invitations for dinner out will shrivel up like microwaved wieners. We'll spend the rest of our lives friendless, but not alone, because we'll have a thousand, million roaches on board to keep us company." I collapsed in a snuffling heap on the settee berth. John sighed, drew me into his arms and patted my back. He gazed thoughtfully into the distance.

"You know," he said gently, "I think you may have a tendency toward over-reaction. Let's go to bed. We'll fumigate in a couple of days."

"A couple of days," I sobbed, "a couple of days. They're reproducing even as we speak."

That night, as I lay rigid and awake beside my gently-snoring husband, I prayed this fervent prayer: "Lord God," I prayed, "Let me not make my poor husband's life a living misery just because I'm having a nervous breakdown because we have roaches. And either blast every single roach into a corpse, or let me learn to like them. Amen."

The next morning, the phone rang early. I grabbed John's arm. "Don't answer that," I whispered.

"Why not?" asked John.

"They've found us," I gasped.

"Who?" asked John.

"The health inspectors," I cried. "They found out about our roaches and they're going to shut us down and we'll be homeless and…"

"Hello?" said John. "Kristy! Well hello! You've broken up with him? Well, he wasn't good enough for you. Of course you can stay with us. Come on over and we'll catch up on old times. About an hour? Wonderful!" John hung up the phone and turned to me. "It's my friend Kristy. Such a lovely girl! I knew her years ago, before I met you."

"Yeah?" I said. "How old is she?"

"Oh, anyone as beautiful as Kristy is practically ageless, but she's about ten years younger than you," he said. "And she's a very clever girl — such a talented artist. You'll really like her."

"I flunked art in grade five," I said. "Where are we going to put her?"

"Oh, Kristy will fit anywhere," said John with a laugh. "She's just a little slip of a girl. She was always so thin. How about the forward cabin?"

"Thin?" I said.

"Oh, the forward cabin will be fine. And to think she's single again," said John. "Well, she probably won't be for long. She attracts men like flies."

"Thin, you say?" I asked. "You said she was thin?"

"That's what I said," said John, "but a couple of months of your cooking should fatten her up."

"Well, it worked on me," I said.

An hour later there was a knock at the boat. Framed in the companionway entrance was a striking young woman with long hair and big eyes. "John? Catherine?" she asked uncertainly. I felt a sudden surge of charity, and I swept her into my arms.

"I'm Catherine," I said. "You poor child. You can stay with us for as long as you like. We've got roaches."

"Such a pity Kristy couldn't stay," I commented to my husband later. "She's a lovely young woman."

"I was surprised she left so quickly," said John. "I'd hoped she'd stay with us for awhile."

"Oh well, you know how it is," I said. "She thought her mother might have more room than us. Now about these roaches…"

We heard a knock. I poked my head up through the companionway, and there was my neighbour. "Catherine!" she said. "I've spotted a roach on my boat. What am I going to do?"

"You know," I said, "We've got them too. Come join us for dinner and we'll discuss strategies and roach spray. We're having Tuna Noodle Surprise."

True Love and Understanding

WHEN YOU LIVE on board a boat with the man you love, you have an opportunity for loving intimacy that goes beyond the bounds of the common way. Proximity, glowing candles in the dim evening, and the cozy feeling that comes with the warmth of a diesel oven — all these things lead one to truly understand one's mate.

It was a cold, wet, windy October evening. It was the kind of evening that would make a landlubber shiver and thank his lucky stars he wasn't at sea. The wind moaned ghostily in the rigging of the *Inuksuk* as she rocked gently on her moorings. Inside the *Inuksuk* the main cabin was warm and comfortable as waves of heat washed over the interior from the Dickenson stove. I lit the oil lamps, and the gentle twelve-volt cabin lights, and watched the yellow glow reflect luxuriously off the polished teak panelling and brass fittings. "This is the life," I said to John. "I think I'd like to have a cup of tea and curl up with a book. Could you turn off the TV and play some Bizet? I feel like a little excitement while I'm reading."

"You have no idea of how to have a good time," said John.

"Reading to Bizet is fun," I said.

"Fun? Fun?" said John. "You think that's fun? Fun is dancing naked on a bar table, getting thrown out of the pub and waking up in a cabbage field. That's fun." I put down my book.

"You were naked on a bar table?" I gasped.

"Well, not naked," John admitted. "And it wasn't a bar table either — it was a championship pool table. That's what they yelled at me when they threw me out of the pub. But I admit to the cabbage field."

"Where was this?" I asked.

"In Germany where I was posted in the late '50s. Did I ever tell you about the time I drove a Mercedes into Holland? I was lucky to escape with my life. That was the time the border guards got mad at me. I was smuggling coffee into Germany. They didn't like that. They shot at me. Luckily those Dutch boys had left enough of the Mercedes that I could gun it through the border."

"They shot at you?" I asked.

"Well yes, but they missed." John said. "No wonder they lost the war."

"And this was fun?" I asked.

"I preferred my leaves to the day to day job of being a private in Her Majesty's army. It was quite boring, really. My friends and I were so bored we built a catamaran."

"That sounds constructive," I said. "What did you do with it?"

"It's probably still in the attic of the barracks," said John reflectively.

"Why did you leave it in the attic?" I asked.

"It was sort of a secret," said John. "The German troops had beautiful wooden furniture, and they were always out on maneuvers marching in formation and shouting at each other, so we borrowed their furniture to build the catamaran and the German army was so efficient, they kept replacing the furniture, so we had a limitless supply of wood for our catamaran."

"You stole their furniture?" I gasped.

"Well, not stole exactly," said John. "We left them the catamaran."

"And that was fun?" I asked.

"It was a pretty good time," said John. "More fun than the time I was nearly arrested for spying."

"How did you nearly get arrested for spying?" I asked.

"I worked all by myself in the map room," said John. "It was pretty dull work. The wall didn't go all the way up to the ceiling, and in the next room all the bigwig generals used to gather to plan World War III. Of course I could hear every word, but it wasn't very interesting. I just minded my own business. After about a year they noticed the wall didn't go all the way up to the ceiling and they tried to arrest me. Wasn't my fault."

"Is there anything else you've never told me?" I asked.

"There was the time I and my buddies were in a pub with some Dutch sailors. They invited us back to their boat and gave us some really great Dutch gin. When I woke up the next morning I was under the captain's table and they were casting off. I think they were headed for Holland. I lit out of there in a hurry. Startled the captain. There's a moral here," he added.

"What on earth could that be?" I asked.

"Never drink with sailors," he said.

"You were a soldier, but you managed to get yourself into quite a lot of trouble," I said.

"That wasn't trouble — it was fun," said John. "You realize of course, the reason why we did all those crazy things was because we didn't have any TV. The youth of today doesn't know how to have fun because they watch too much TV."

"Darling," I said.

"Yes?" said John

"When we go offshore, can we strike a balance between Bizet and getting shot at?"

"Whatever you like, my little Snoggy Lips," said John.

Of such delightful compromises are marriages made.

Fitness for the Sailor

"**I HAVE GIVEN** some thought to my girth," I told my husband, "and I have decided to do something about it." I thoughtfully took a bite out of a cookie. "Since we're too broke to join a gym, I've developed a series of exercise routines suitable for the sailor." I handed John a sheet of paper. "Feast your eyes on this," I said, "while I whip up a crock pot cake for dessert tonight."

1. Leaving-the-Dock Sprint: This exercise involves the use of a pike pole. The crewmember runs up and down the deck with a pike pole, offering affectionate words of advice to the Captain as the boat leaves the dock. If the tide and wind catch the boat broadside and send the boat floundering around the marina, the Crew can burn extra calories requesting help from the owners of the docked boats, most of whom are more than happy to assist.

2. Hauling-Lines Squat: The minute the Captain orders the Crew to "raise the main," the Crew must ascertain which sail this is. Then she must choose a likely-looking line and pull on it in a fluid motion, squatting close to the deck at the end of each pull. This exercise should be approached with caution by those crewmembers who are over 45.

If she finds she is unable to rise out of the crouch position, she may pull herself up by way of the line and the mast. Any Captain who has more than two masts should have more than one crewmember, particularly if the Crew is nearing menopause.

3. Dropping-Anchor Foot Flexion: It takes skill to perform this exercise. When the Captain gives the command, the Crew releases the anchor lever, sending the anchor and chain hurtling downward. The crewmember places her (shod) foot over the top of the chain, preventing the chain from jumping its housing and fouling. By dexterously changing feet, the Crew can give equal play to both legs. When the Captain yells, "What in heaven's name are you doing hopping around like that? Got bugs?" ignore him. You want toned legs, and a little ridicule must not dissuade you.

4. Weighing-Anchor Lunge: This one is a full body workout. Someone short who was probably a man designed our manual winch system. There's a short lever you have to pull back and forth, but to get to it you have to squat close to the deck with one foot on each side of the Danforth anchor that seems to be there for decoration, and lurch backwards and forwards in a rhythmic movement. The Captain asks every few feet of chain if the anchor's broken loose yet. You naturally want to know what foolish person authorized the letting out of these hundreds of feet of chain, and a lively discussion ensues between Captain and Crew, taking your mind off the racking pain in your body.

5. Docking Long-Jump: As the boat nears the dock, the Crew readies herself in anticipation of the leap from the deck to

the dock that must inevitably ensue. A line must be carried during this exercise. The motivation to perform well is persuasive: any shortfalls result in sudden post-exercise ablutions. It is of great comfort to me to know that portly people tend to float in salt water.

"And what," John asked, "does the Captain do for exercise while the Crew is enjoying her luxurious on board spa treatment?"

"Oh, that's easy," I replied, and handed him a second sheet.

1. Pike-Pole Chase and Boat-Fending Thrust: While the panicked Crew is racing up and down the deck with the pike pole, the Captain must steer the boat, chase the crewmember, recover the pike pole and fend the boat off other boats in the marina.

2. Deck Race: As the Crew is dancing from one foot to another during the execution of the Dropping-Anchor Foot Flexion, the Captain is responsible for running back and forth between the wheel and the bow to ensure the anchor is being set properly.

3. Dinghy Boat Row: Just before the Crew executes the Weighing-Anchor Lunge, the Captain recovers the stern line with the dinghy, always bearing in mind that the crewmember left in charge of the boat longer than three minutes is a nervous crewmember.

4. Recovery of Object in Water Dive-and-Swim: In the event of a shortfall in the Docking Long-Jump, the Captain is responsible for a) saving the life of the Crew, and b) ensuring the stern line she's dropped does not foul the prop. Which of these tasks does he perform first? The answer is

complex and will vary between boats.

John looked up from the paper. "Excellent," he said. "I feel thinner already. What's for supper?"

"Something delicious, my darling," I said. "And after dessert we can watch that exercise video I bought at the thrift store. But no cheating — we have to sit up while it's on."

107

Hail and Farewell

FRIENDS AND NEIGHBOURS, I want to thank you for inviting us to this farewell get-together. John and I have spent three wonderful years in Cowichan Bay living on board the *Inuksuk*, and we will treasure our memories. We're headed off to be the Dooks of Sooke. As you know, we sail tomorrow. That scarecrow figure of "First Mate Murphy" you put on our bow would make a terrific figurehead, but I think I'd rather leave him behind. No offense.

Since most of you have at one time or another towed us back into Cowichan Bay, I want to take this opportunity to express my appreciation. Some of you have scanned the horizon anxiously to make sure we made it safely out of the harbour, some of you have leaped to fend us off the boats we've nearly hit as we've floundered around the marina, some of you have caught lines when we've been towed into our slip trailing smoke, and some of you have fired up your engines and come looking for us when we've broken down, lost our bearings or melted our engine. When we couldn't make it past Cape Keppel in two years of trying, you blamed it on the Cape. When we clipped our neighbour's bow while docking, you said it could've happened to anyone. When our engine broke down, you blamed it on "Crewmember Murphy." You stood by your radios in anxious anticipation of our next "pan-pan" call and offered nothing but constructive, helpful advice. I remember fondly how two of you proved with a salt shaker, a teaspoon and three napkins how easy it would be to saw six inches off our boom, raise the cockpit a foot and install a single sideband radio with a cement saw. We can't wait to try out all your suggestions. We were novices when we got here, and thanks to your support, advice and boat-towing expertise, we always made it home. If it were not for you wonderful folks, we'd be floating around out there contracting scurvy. We think you're great.

My girlfriends have been terrific. The time we painted our deck brown and the hull blue, you were kind. When I asked questions like, "So what's that rope for?" you explained. When I tried to fasten the boat with a running spring line, you didn't make fun of me. You showed me how to tie a bowline, took me for walks, laughed at my jokes and didn't spurn my cooking. You explained that men never ask for directions and advised me to study celestial navigation "just in case." You told me my hair looked nice the month I gained two pounds on the Bannock Diet. You gave me recipes perfect for a diesel oven and told me those cookies weren't my fault at all. You explained how many pounds of turkey can be crammed into a pressure cooker and which parts you have to rip off to make it fit. You told me about the time you lashed a broken rudder to your boat with a length of line and sailed back single-handed from Genoa Bay. We have dwelt at length on the subject of the nature of husbands, and though the issue is not yet settled, the debate has given us hours of pleasure.

You are all our friends. One last time we ask you to stand by your radios. One last time we ask you to gaze toward Cape Keppel looking for smoke. One last time, and we are gone until next year.

But remember this, and hold it close to your heart. Wherever we sail, we shall take a little bit of Cowichan Bay with us. We've got roaches.

We love you, we'll miss you, and God bless.

By the way, does anybody here know where I can get my hands on some DDT?

The Exterminator (Postscript)

J OHN IS THE most optimistic person I know. And amazingly, he's usually right. When the engine light goes on he says, "Engine's never been better. I can tell by the way it sounds. The light must have a faulty wire." When the bilge alarm goes off twice in an hour he says, "Good! Shows it's working!" When we don't recognize features on the chart, John says, "I know exactly where we are. This chart must be outdated." But the most amazingly optimistic thing I've ever head him say was this: "We only saw one roach. Maybe it died."

This one time, John was wrong. And as that little (obviously pregnant) roach escaped from our view, we went through the classic grief reaction. Denial ("Are you sure it was a roach?"), rage ("This must be someone's fault!"), despair ("We'll never get rid of them — never, never, never") and resignation ("Maybe we'll get to like them. The babies are kind of cute"). Or at least I did — John was watching TV.

"Have you done emoting?" asked John, as the final credits to "The Simpsons" came up on the screen. I was collapsed in a quivering heap. Slowly I rose to my feet. I raised my clenched fist.

"As God is my witness," I intoned, "I will never have roaches again." There was a gleam in my eye, defiance in my jaw and a carrot in my fist. I took a bite. "Tomorrow," I said, "we phone an exterminator."

"We can't afford an exterminator," said John.

"Darling," I said reasonably, "we can't afford not to. Everyone knows the only way to get rid of roaches is to hire an exterminator. Doing it yourself — what, that way lies madness. Everything is stacked in favour of the roaches. They're faster than we are, there are more of them, and they're probably smarter. After all, roaches don't watch "Who Wants to be a Millionaire.""

"Very funny," said John. "But we still can't afford an exterminator."

"Oh, all right," I said. "Tomorrow we'll dress to blend and skulk around the discount bins at Canadian Tire."

We discovered something as we made our way unobtrusively around the local pesticide displays. Asking questions about how to rid a boat of roaches had the same effect as the ringing bell did in the Middle Ages, or the scarlet letter two centuries ago. Young, initially friendly salespersons manifested reactions ranging from fear to revulsion to the curled lip. I smiled and recalled with a sigh my own young adulthood, when I'd been heard to say things like, "No child of mine will ever behave like that in public!" Ah, the intolerance of youth! Considering how God had dealt with my own case, I shuddered to think what was in store for these young sales clerks.

Clutching two sets of smoke bombs, four bottles of chemical guaranteed to kill bugs if you hit them in the face with the spray, some expensive roach traps and a gross of bait, we hurried back to the *Inuksuk*.

We were quietly optimistic. We spoke in calm, quiet tones — measured and confident. Our bearing was not unlike that of a general before a major campaign. Montcalm, say, surveying the plains of Abraham, or Napoleon sizing up Waterloo, or General Lee, for example, taking a look at Gettysburg.

Yes, we thought we could win.

We started with the galley. "I'll throw out all our food," I said, "while you rip up the floorboards."

"What?" asked John, "the marmite and mint sauce too?"

"We'll leave nothing for them to eat, darling," I said patiently.

"And what do we eat while we're starving the roaches?" John asked.

"Stop arguing and help me rip the boat apart," I said. "Then we spray, bomb and plant bait."

Three days later, we were hungry and dishevelled. There was a thick pall of noxious chemicals in the air. Our boat looked as though we'd weathered a typhoon and the boat had pitchpoled once or twice. Our possessions lay scattered in heaps around our calves. But all was not lost — we'd killed at least 11 roaches. There was a grim set to my jaw.

John looked at me appealingly. "Can we eat today?" he asked humbly.

"Darling," I said, and I flung my arms around his neck. "I've neglected you horribly. Let's go to the grocery store and I'll buy you some bread and marmite. And beans. I think we have cause to celebrate."

We slept well that night, and when I woke the next morning, I noticed that the view was wonderful and the air fresh and clean. Such exhilaration and happiness swelled in my breast. John too was filled with happiness. But our joy was fleeting. Two days later when I was standing in the galley, a small insect sprinted from one end of the counter to another. I killed him with a four-pound frying pan, simultaneously emitting a battle cry that sent neighbouring seagulls skyward in protesting flocks.

"Darling," I said after I'd restored myself, "wouldn't you prefer to have a pleasant, sane wife? Do let's phone an exterminator — there's a dear."

Wordlessly John handed me the cell phone. Defeat is a terrible thing.

His name was Blair, of Abell Pest Control, and he came from Victoria in an hour. It took him thirty minutes to lay bait throughout the boat, and we didn't have to empty a single locker or rip up one floorboard. John and I were flabbergasted at how easy it was. "You mean that's all?" I asked, "and you guarantee your work?"

"Every roach," he said kindly. "Phone me if you have any problems." He handed us his card. I have it still.

Wordlessly, we clasped his hand in parting. His discreetly-labelled truck disappeared into the mist.

I wondered what would have been the outcome of history if Montcalm had boasted a Blair in his ranks…or Lee, or Napoleon? I love my husband, but every now and then you meet a figure larger than life. He came into our lives, and then he had to leave. I turned to my husband. "John," I said, "Let's shop for groceries. I shall cook you a roast with Yorkshire pudding."

"And Spotty Dick?" asked John.

"Now then, darling," I said, "You know I've always said the raisins look too much like bugs…"

"You can relax now," said John confidently. "I told you we'd get rid of the roaches. And I'm usually right about these things."

"Of course you are, darling," I said.

Post Postscript

"**D**ARLING, IT'LL BE Valentine's Day soon," I said. "This may be leading up to something," said John. "What would you like?"

"Well, my sweet," I said, "do you remember that charming fairy tale where two of the daughters asked for jewels and fine dresses and Beauty asked for a red rose?"

"Oh, I remember the story," said John. "You'd like a red rose?"

"It was the red rose that caused all the trouble," I said. "I'd prefer the jewels and fine dresses. Size eighteen."

"We'll celebrate with half a Mars bar by candlelight," said John. "I budgeted for it specially."

"You're so romantic, darling," I said. "Do you remember when we first moved on board together?"

"I remember as if it were yesterday," said John. "You made me install an electric head. Cost me a fortune."

"You said at the time it was worth every penny to see me happy," I said. "And remember when you clasped me in your arms and you told me you didn't want me to give up one thing I valued when we moved on board?"

"That was before I knew you owned three hundred books," said John glumly.

"Yes, my darling," I said. "We've been deliriously happy on board for three years now. Do you remember our first meals on the boat?"

"Clearly," said John. "That was before you learned to adjust the carburetor drip on the diesel stove, and the first week you burned everything to cinders. But I knew you had greatness in you, and the potatoes have been edible ever since."

"And those walks we took arm in arm down the docks? Ropes and wires and dog dirt underfoot, the sharp tang of diesel exhaust and wood smoke, barking pit bulls and a scattering of cats?"

"Yes, my little dumpling," said John.

"We were newly in love, then, and at the periphery of the busy social hub of Cowichan Bay. After a couple of months, the lad who lives on the tug told us that after careful research he'd decided we'd make the best parents on the dock. 'Mom? Dad?' he said, 'what's for dinner?' And those leisurely cups of coffee we shared at the Bluenose! After the first year the waitress stopped asking us if we were going to order breakfast too. Those magical moments when we dug into the change jar looking for enough quarters to do the laundry. The pub songs you sang to me when I was fired…"

"I don't remember any singing," said John.

"Robin Hood, Robin Hood, riding through the glen
Robin Hood, Robin Hood, with his merry men
Feared by the good, he loved Christmas pud
Robin Hood, Robin Hood, Robin Hood."

"Oh," said John.

"Those times the docks broke up and you gallantly held the flashlight for me while I crawled across two boards lashed together on my hands and knees? Remember those happy times?"

116

"I remember what you said about the docks," said John. "In fact, it's seared on my brain."

"Darling," I said.

"Yes dear?" said John.

"We may not have Paris, but we'll always have Cowichan Bay."

"Yes, my little dumpling," he said. "We'll always have Cowichan Bay."

Games for Liveaboards

"**D**ODGING DRIPS" **IS** one of the sports you take up when you live aboard. Show me a boat, and I'll show you a source of drips. And the drip in summer is the winter monsoon that requires wearing hip waders to bed.

A corollary to the "dodging drips" game is the "finding out where the drips are coming from" game. My husband is particularly fond of this one. Every rainstorm will find him crawling around the main saloon with a flashlight, muttering to himself. I have learned that there are no winners in this game, nor does it ever end. Sitting comfortably in the corner with a book, I suggest that we not attempt to Sikoflex in spots like we've been doing — that we Sikoflex the entire deck to the depth of an inch or so and then paint on top. This suggestion is met with hostile looks, so I return to my book.

Another pastime is called "going to the head at midnight." On board the *Inuksuk*, this ordeal means bending double through the passageway from the aft cabin to the main saloon. The floor is slanted there, and he who is unwary or half asleep falls into the engine room. This denotes instant forfeit of the game. The passageway is only stage one, or the base stage. Stage two, or the median stage, is negotiating the main saloon in the dark, where one's wife may have dropped her clothing or the laundry. Should the player slip or stumble on any such obstacles, the confrontation is accompanied by spirited shouts highly amusing to the partner still in bed. Having successfully made passage through the main saloon, the player, excited by his nearly successful completion of the odyssey, rushes into the head proper, or apex stage, where he is confronted by a freezing cold head and one of two variations, depending on the sex of the player. Should the player be male, he may find the floor covered with icy water where his wife didn't clean up after her shower. The female player may find the toilet seat up and she falls into the head. The trip back is anti-climactic and hardly worth mentioning — sort of like climbing back down Mount Everest. The winning player is able to either negotiate the hazards without losing his temper or wake up his partner and make her feel guilty.

A fourth game is called "deciding who will change the sheets on the aft cabin berth." He who changes the sheets in the aft cabin has to crawl on his belly over top of the bedding with an eighteen-inch headspace towards the foot of the berth, wrestle with the aft corners, and rip the sheets off and drag them back with him, avoiding tangling with a couple of blankets and a duvet. Naturally, there is some polite jostling to avoid this job. John has made use of such tactics as questioning the necessity of doing it at all. "It's not spring yet," he says. This game hones negotiation skills. Emotional blackmail is permitted, but inventing back injuries is cheating. Similar skirmishes, in ascending order of intensity, are called "deciding who scrubs the deck" and "determining if the bilge needs cleaning."

Another game we play is called "finding the neighbour's cat." There are two purposes for this game. One is to encourage Buddy (the cat) to leave if we're going someplace for an extended period, and the other is to read his collar. The neighbours have their phone number written there, and I can never remember it. Buddy prefers either the down duvet in the forward cabin or the Hudson's Bay point blanket in the aft cabin, but I've found him sleeping in the locker above the stove, curled next to the dinner plates. I'm proud that Buddy approves of my taste in furnishings.

A particularly entertaining pastime is called "what's that noise?" This is most effective after dark. It requires acute hearing on the part of one of the players, and is the most fun if the other partner is asleep. A pump goes off, followed by a small click and then silence. What happened? Did the battery charger kick in and blow the breakers, or did the freezer compressor start and then change its mind? If the breakers are blown, the freezer will melt a week's groceries and the bilge pumps will be non-functional by morning, possibly causing the boat to sink should that seacock we can't find suddenly spring a leak and the boat fill up with water and…"John, John! Wake up! Why is it quiet?" This kind of question falls into the highest possible category and is worth maximum points. We often used to play this game when we first moved on board the *Inuksuk*.

The mental stimulation accorded liveaboards keeps us alert and happy. I'm sure the longer we're liveaboards the more games we'll find to play. In fact, just the other morning we invented "make John change his socks."

Deck the Deck

"**D**ECK THE DECK with boughs of holly, fa la la la la, la la la la" I sang.

"Bah! Humbug!" said my husband.

"Deck the bloke who isn't jolly, fa la la la la, la la la la." I continued. "Don we now our favourite blue jeans, fa la la, la la la, la la la. Feast we now on eggs and canned beans, fa la la la la, la la la la."

John scowled at me. "It's Halloween," he said. "You have your seasons all mixed up."

"It's not," I said defensively. "Canadian Tire had a Christmas display up in mid-October. It's been Christmas for ages. Halloween is long gone, and now 'tis the season to be jolly."

"Halloween has been gone for 24 hours," said my husband.

"Out with the old and up with the tree," I said. "Now where did I put the Christmas decorations? A little tinsel will really brighten this place up."

"Tinsel?" gasped my husband. "This is a boat! Pirates don't have tinsel."

"Pirates don't have legally married wives ' 'til death do us part,' either, darling," I said. "Come now — don't you like plum pudding?"

"Well, yes," said John.

"And candied carrots with ginger?"

"I concede the point," said John.

"And turkey?"

"I do like turkey," he said.

"And presents?"

"Presents are good," he admitted. "What are you getting me?"

"It's a secret," I said. "If you let me put up a tree, I'll give you something nice."

"There's no room on board for a tree," he said.

"Of course there is, darling," I said. "I'll just put the TV in storage and…"

"What?" asked John.

"The TV, darling," I said, "And some of these radios, too, I think. They're awfully in the way. You don't mind, do you? And how about you put some twinkly lights up on the mast and all around the stanchions? And a plastic Santa on the deck?"

"You've got to be kidding," said John.

"Actually, I am," I said. "The clever wife will not hesitate to play a little highball-lowball when the stakes are a Christmas tree. You can keep the TV, but I do want a tree. A little one, with lights." John sank back against the cushions, relief stamped on his face like a tattoo.

"Whatever you say, Catherine," he said, "but no boat lights, and no plastic Santa."

"Done!" I exclaimed, and I raced off to storage to dig out the decorations.

Our twelve-inch tree stood on the top of the TV on top of the navigation table opposite the galley. After the tree was up, I quietly sneaked a handful of red fabric poinsettias into one of the glasses sitting against the forward cabin wall. A few days later I put my miniature crèche on the table in the main saloon and reverently arranged the little pieces. After that I became bolder, and one day I strung a line of winking lights across the deck head. John finally felt moved to protest. "Christmas is crowding us out of our boat," he said. "Every time the wind blows and the boat rocks, that little tree falls on the floor and sprays decorations and tinsel in all directions. Yesterday one of the wise men fell into my potatoes while I was trying to eat dinner, and those lights distract me while I watch TV. All this shortbread is giving me indigestion, and the constant Christmas carols are getting on my nerves. Can't you go back to 'Sweating to the Oldies'? Richard Simmons is much more interesting than Santa Claus. Before I married you I thought Christmas lasted one day — I didn't realize the season could be dragged out for two months."

"Remember what happened to Scrooge," I said loftily. "Besides, I'm getting you boat stuff for Christmas." I began to sing, "Oh, star of wonder, star of light. Celestial navigation's all right. Nonetheless a GPS will guide us safely through the night."

"Boat stuff?" John asked. He reached for another piece of shortbread. "Cute little tree," he said, "and I'm getting used to tinsel dangling in front of the TV screen." He joined in. "We three sailors down at the dock. Everything we own is in hock. While we're sailing, reverently praying the boat doesn't strike a rock."

"You always get your way, don't you?" he asked. "Why is that, I wonder. For fifty-seven years I thought I could think for myself, and then I married you and now I realize I was doing it all wrong. Merry Christmas, Catherine."

"Merry Christmas, darling," I said. "Only one month to go."

Cooking on Board

I'M IN LOVE with my husband, but he thinks instant mashed potatoes are food. John spent thirty-five years living in Canada's Arctic. He went through a "kill it and eat it raw" phase, a "buy it from the Hudson's Bay Company" phase, and a "grow it yourself in the musket" phase that fortunately he'd outgrown by the time I met him. Since the discharge of firearms is discouraged at Cowichan Bay and garden space is limited on the docks, we rely on the bewildering array of choices to be found at Superstore. Because of John's early deprivation as a customer of the Hudson's Bay Company, we walk right past the kiwi fruit and smoked salmon and come home every week with bananas, canned beans and instant mashed potatoes.

One of John's arguments is that our refrigeration is limited on board the *Inuksuk*. He has a point. We have no fridge on board, but we do own a built-in freezer the size of a small car. Unfortunately, it freezes solid and then thaws into mush, turning every meal into a round of "bacteria roulette." Add to this John's declaration that his English ancestors traditionally repelled invaders by feeding them, and one can see why I'd volunteer to do the cooking. Just watching John wield a salt shaker gives me an irregular heartbeat. There are those in my past who would say Canada too is safe as long as I have access to an oven, but I'm a deft hand with a can opener, and I know my way around a vegetable.

We use the deck as our refrigerator in the spring and fall. In winter and summer we eat perishables in one sitting. There is a deep, cool locker alongside the oven where I store (real) potatoes and onions, and a locker above the freezer where I store canned goods. Behind the diesel oven is another locker for dishes and dry goods. There's not much space for imaginative groceries. We rely on staples — the kinds of staples you could buy from the Hudson's Bay Company store in a small Arctic community 30 years ago. Refrigeration and space were issues then, as they are aboard the *Inuksuk*. We have come full circle.

"What's for dinner?" John asks.

"Modified chicken cordon bleu on a bed of rice with a side of steamed vegetables and salad and a glass of wine," I say. "I think the chicken is safe — it was frozen, but then so was the cheese. I salvaged the last of the carrots from the potato locker — they're starting to grow hair — and I had to dig for the wine. It was at the bottom of the dry goods locker under the instant mashed potatoes. I had to fight the neighbourhood cats for the head of lettuce I'd left on the deck and the rice I borrowed from the neighbours."

"Where's the beans?" John asks.

You see what I'm up against? I have no idea why John prefers beans when I go to all the trouble of preparing elegant meals. Still, there are worse things than cooking for a man with a plain palate. John doesn't notice that a dramatic culinary failure is a failure. Charcoal passes by unremarked, and peculiar casseroles are eaten with the same appreciation as Christmas dinner. Unfailingly polite, John eats whatever I put in front of him. I'm glad I listened to my brother-in-law when he said, "The way you cook and the way he eats, God has sent you this man. Marry him."

Total Woman in Training

ONE OF THE real advantages to living on a boat is that you're always so broke buying boat parts that you do all your personal shopping in thrift stores and auctions, thereby increasing your quality of life by exposing yourself to all kinds of wonderful junk that you try to talk your husband into storing on board. One particularly valuable "find" was a 25-cent copy of *The Total Woman*. Remember the Total Woman? The Total Woman, so the book tells us, is responsible for being submissive to her husband at all times, apologizing every time he sulks and surprising him by wearing little "outfits" when she meets him at the door after work. I hadn't read the book when it came out in the '70s. During that period I wore a "Why Not" button and bawled out professors who made sexist jokes. But now it was the new millennium and I'd actually landed a real husband. Maybe the author knew something I didn't. I was short on outfits, so I decided to improvise. I put a plastic bag on top of my head and danced in the main saloon. "That book should be called 'The Total Nut,'" said my beloved.

"Your reaction is all wrong, darling," I said. "According to chapter six, you're supposed to melt into my arms and give me garnets for Christmas."

"You're blocking my view of the television," said John. Obviously, the book was mistaken. I stacked it in a pile of things to put into storage the next time I made a trip up the dock and forgot about it.

Later that afternoon, John approached me. "Catherine," he said, "my friend down the dock wants to take his power boat for a run this afternoon to test the motor. I'd like to go with him."

"Oh no," I said. "He's just as bad as you are. The engine is sure to break down and you'll both be convinced you can fix it, and you'll never think of calling the Coast Guard for help and you'll be stuck out there for weeks, drifting back and forth with the tide, eating fish and drinking rainwater. People will say, 'Where's your husband?' and I'll have to tell them, 'He's floating around Cowichan Bay with his friend because they're both too proud to ask for help.' Besides, who'll fix the head when you're out having fun?"

When we bought the head it was expensive enough, but since the Canadian dollar went through the macerator, the repair kit now costs as much as the head did originally, and the head itself has appreciated in Canadian dollars to the extent that when I sit on it I feel like a queen. I bet even the royal family doesn't pee into a toilet as expensive as ours. "But I'd feel even more like royalty if the head worked," I told John. "So you can't go out on any mad excursions until you've left your wife with a working head."

"The Total Woman would be grateful for a bucket," said my husband. "And the Total Woman would let her husband drift around in circles in Cowichan Bay for as long as he liked. She'd put a plastic bag on top of her head and row out in her little dinghy to bring him hot chicken dinners." The book was backfiring on me. "You're obviously not a successful Total Woman yet," he said. "You're only a Total Woman in Training."

"That spells TWIT," I said.

"If the plastic bag fits..." he said loftily. This was shaping into an ugly situation. Where was the sweet man who said, "Yes, dear" every time I asked him to repair something? Where was the man who fried dinner and fixed instant mashed potatoes whenever I couldn't face the galley and then did the washing-up afterward? Who wiped the dribbles off the table and did the laundry?

"Wait a minute," I said, "it doesn't say anything in *The Total Woman* about the wife holding down a full-time job and supporting her husband in luxury and boat parts." There was silence.

"You're right, dear," said my husband. He fixed the head and then went for his jaunt without incident.

I went from being a TWIT back to being first mate, and I mailed the book as a Christmas present to my most liberated girlfriend. It's amazing what you can find in thrift stores.

Tell us a Story, John

ONE VERY ANCIENT and graceful art at which most live-aboards excel is that of storytelling. We come from all walks of life, and the cumulative experiences of our lives touch a range and breadth not found in just any group. The exotic rhythms of the ocean and the quiet lapping of the waves in the mysterious dark lend themselves to the natural fluency of the raconteur. Besides, there's nothing on TV.

Let's eavesdrop while John tells a story about the Arctic.

"Friend of mine was a Netsilik Eskimo. His mother went insane and there was no RCMP, no nurse, nobody to do anything about it. The community decided she had to be shot."

"Oh my God," gasped my neighbour. "The poor woman was obviously going through menopause."

"Yeah," I said. "Or PMS. A little PMS and someone shoots you. More coffee?" We were visiting in the main saloon of the *Inuksuk* — our neighbour, John and I. It was warm and we were enjoying the quiet of the evening.

"I'll never admit to another hot flash," said my neighbour.

John ignored us and soldiered on. "They said since my friend was the closest relative, he had to shoot the poor mad woman."

"Does John own a gun?" asked my neighbour.

"John is a strict pacifist," I said. "The closest he's ever come to violence is the time he came home with a rose for me. I asked him where he got it and he said that he'd mugged a 'Take Back the Night' marcher and stolen her rose. The closest I've ever come to violence was our first anniversary. John gave me a copy of *PCs for Dummies*."

"No!" said my friend, "And you let him live?"

"I kicked up such a fuss, I got pearls the following Christmas," I said. "But he regressed the very next anniversary, and I scored a wooden spoon."

"May I finish my story?" asked John.

"Of course, my darling," I said.

John continued. "So my friend killed his own mother, and he had the gratitude of the entire Netsilik village."

"They shot her just like Old Yeller," I said.

"Years later," said John, "my friend accidentally caught his right arm in some machinery and tore it off."

"John tells good stories, wouldn't you say?" I asked brightly. "Cake, anyone?"

"Thanks, I'm not hungry just now," said my neighbour.

"I asked him how he was making out without his arm," continued John. "And he said he was very happy — the arm he lost had held the rifle that killed his mother, and now her spirit was avenged."

"Are you going offshore with this man?" asked my neighbour.

"Never a dull anecdote," I said. "I first fell in love with him when his boss said that most of John's stories ended with him going to jail. I knew right then John was no ordinary raconteur."

"John darling," I said, "tell our neighbour about the man you knew who worked for NASA and as an experiment grew edible fungus on his arm as food for astronauts."

My neighbour threw up her hands. "I think you two deserve each other. For goodness sake, let's see what's on TV."

Mildew is an Earth Tone

"**D**ARLING," I SAID, "my clothing locker drips."
"It's your imagination," said John. "It's condensation."
"Feel this," I said, thrusting a wettish sweatshirt sleeve under my beloved's nose.

"Damp, isn't it?" said John. "My, but you must sweat a lot."

"Darling," I said, "he who drills holes in the deck over a locker causes said locker to drip. You put a whole set of handrails six feet long along the deck, and now my entire wardrobe is growing fungus. My beautiful hand knit socks are little musty fur balls, my T-shirts are all damp and my jeans have a fine green sheen. I have to launder everything in close rotation just to keep the smell down."

"So the solution is more water, not less," said John. I gave up.

Every morning I choose another designer outfit for the day. If I don't recognize the crumpled mass that slides off the hanger onto the aft cabin floor, I dispose of it and choose another item. During a heavy rain, I am sometimes ankle deep in former favourites before I can find something wearable. "How about this green T-shirt?" I mutter to myself. "No — wait — didn't the matching slacks develop a fungus problem last week?

Well, how about this blouse? No — it needs ironing and I've temporarily misplaced the iron under a stack of books and sock yarn. I bet I could wear the green T-shirt with jeans, if I could find a dry pair of jeans." I hastily rifle through my locker, looking for jeans. Yes — there — crammed next to a rumpled, rust-coloured suit jacket. Oh rats! They're wet. I balance my desire to get dressed against the discomfort of wearing damp jeans and decide in favor of the jeans. "Oh no," I moan, "I left the sock drawer open again, and that leak through the dorade directly above the open drawer has turned my favourite socks to mush." I find another pair in an alternative colour — bright yellow — anything goes with sneakers — and as an after-thought, I grab the suit jacket, hoping no one will notice the wrinkles.

"How do I look?" I ask my husband.

"Wonderful," he says. "I think you've lost weight."

Satisfied, I move on to the head, where I search through my make-up case looking for lipstick that will go with blue, rust, green and neon yellow. It's a daunting task. I plan another trip to Value Village. "We have to go," I tell my husband. "After all, my clothing locker drips."

"It's your imagination," says John. "To change the subject, I think I'll build a bolted-down cabinet for the generator on deck just above the aft cabin. Now where did I stow my hammer drill?"

Live Graciously

IT WAS THREE years ago. I was standing on the dock in Cowichan Bay in my high heels talking to a little man in stained pants and a rumpled shirt who had the brightest eyes I'd ever seen. "Live graciously," he said kindly, bestowing a sparkling look on me. "Throw out everything you own that's tin and plastic, and bring out the crystal and china and silver. You don't need junk on board your boat. You need to use the best you own. Real duck down duvets, the nicest clothes, the best linens and clean tea towels. Polish up your brass and enjoy your lifestyle. Why, I even have a bathtub on my boat," he said with a smile. His little dog, smart and loyal, ran towards him as he turned to leave. "Remember what I said," he repeated, "live graciously."

I found out later the little dog had been bathless nearly his entire canine career, and the bathtub was full of tools, but I never forgot his message or his face bright with happiness.

So I spent thirty-two dollars on two hand-woven tea towels. "What?" said John.

"If I can only have two tea towels, my love," I told him, "I want it to be these two. Space is limited on board a boat, and one must have the very best."

"Oh very well," said John, reaching for a tea towel.

"Don't touch it," I snapped. John drew his hand back and looked bewildered.

"Why not?" he asked. "I was going to wipe my hands."

"Are they clean?" I asked.

"Of course they're clean — I just washed them," said John.

"Let me see your fingernails," I said.

"I'll wipe my hands on my pants. Will that make you happy?" John asked. "What are we going to use these tea towels for, exactly? Can we wipe dishes with them?"

"Well, no — they're too nice to actually use," I said. "I think we'll just look at them. My, they look nice." I stepped back and cocked my head admiringly.

"You must be joking," said John. "Nobody spends thirty-two dollars on something to look at. I used to own an art gallery, so I know these things. I nearly starved to death, but the bailiff cut my misery short and I was able to get a job before the art gallery killed me." He pulled a tea towel out of its brass ring and defiantly wiped his hands on it. "I want to get my thirty-two dollars worth," he said.

"Oh, all right darling," I said, "but no wiping dishes with them — please?"

"What are we going to wipe our dishes with if these little artifacts are off limits?" John asked.

I held up a torn grey rag with some stitching along one side. "Genuine hand embroidery, darling," I said. "Live graciously."

"I'm not sure I'd want that thing to touch the engine, let alone the dishes," said John.

"Oh, all right. I'll toss it," I said, "but my heart isn't in it." I took out John's family heirloom pewter candelabra, placed it on my favourite placemat and stood back to admire the effect. "Doesn't it look lovely, darling?" I said. John reached toward the candles with a lighter. "Don't light those," I said sharply.

"Why not?" asked John, startled.

"The wax might drip on my placemat," I replied, "or dribble down the side of the candelabra."

John lit the candles.

"Live graciously," he said. "Not 'look as though you're living graciously.'" I paused thoughtfully.

"I think you may be right, darling," I said. "I've never been reckless with beautiful things before, but now may be the time. After all, when do you really start living? Tonight we dine on china and use our genuine gold-edged mugs. Tonight we sleep under our goose down duvet. And tomorrow I'll put on my prettiest sweater and best slacks and buy the most exotic groceries we can afford. Live graciously."

"Can we still buy beans?" asked John.

"Of course, my darling," I said, "but you may have to eat them with a silver fork."

"I don't mind living graciously if I can still have beans," said John. "And can I store my tools in the head?"

"Only if they all match, darling," I said. "I'll have to get you some new ones in coordinated colours for Christmas. Any colour preferences in mind?"

"You know," said John, "I've always been grateful you've never tended towards inscribed cufflinks for presents. I'll go for blue or yellow — your choice."

"Even I know there are limits to gracious living on board a boat," I said. "Cufflinks! How silly! Now where did I stow my nosebleed spikes..."

Christmas Aboard

"IT'S NEARLY CHRISTMAS, darling," I said rapturously. "I can hardly wait to invite the entire family over for dinner."

"There's no room," said John.

"No room!" I gasped. "What a thing to say! Why, we have forty-four feet of living space! Private cabins for visitors! A head with shower room for two! Every luxury of living space you can imagine, and room for a tree, if we rearrange the TV a trifle."

"Change that to 'private cabin for visitors,'" John said repressively, "and there are an awful lot of Dooks."

"So whose fault is that?" I said. "When God said, 'Go forth and multiply,' he wasn't talking about just you."

"Six kids," I continued ecstatically, "and eight grandchildren."

"Nine," said John.

"Oh — I'd forgotten Mikey," I said. "He's brand new, but he's just as cute as his granddaddy." I pinched John on the cheek.

"He doesn't look anything like me," said John. "He's short, he dresses funny, he's beardless and he hasn't even got a job yet."

"So," I said, "not to change the subject or anything, but how many family members can we expect?"

"None," said John. "If we don't invite anybody, there'll be more turkey for us."

"I'm going to ignore that," I said. "Nunavut can't do without Jackie, and Maggie can't make it down from Yellowknife. Paul's coming from Edmonton. Lisa and Lito and Mikey should be able to make it from Vancouver, and John Jr.'s only in Cowichan Bay. Has there been a Rupert sighting recently?"

"Rupert appears to be buzzing back and forth between Fort Smith and Yellowknife," said John, "but Maggie said he was taking flying lessons in Edmonton for awhile."

"Expect the unexpected," I said. "If his truck holds out, we can probably count on him sometime between now and Mother's Day. We'll have to stock up on peach jam — it's his favourite."

"We have a locker full of peach jam," said John grumpily. "There'll be no room left for presents."

"I wonder if John Jr. will bring his kitten," I continued. "We should make room for a portable litter box."

"Don't want kittens," said John. "I want daughters-in-law."

"Now you're getting into the Christmas spirit," I said approvingly. "But a kitten is what we've got."

"We'll have to put Paul in the forward cabin," I continued, counting off my fingers, "and Lisa and Lito in the main saloon with Mikey. John Jr. can sleep on the floor on a foam mattress, you and I will have the aft cabin, and the cat can sleep with Paul. The litter box we'll fit in the head, the diaper bag will go in the galley, and we'll restrict everyone to one change of clothing in a gym bag."

"That's four gym bags!" exclaimed John.

"No problem, darling," I said. "I've got the perfect plan. We'll pile them in the passageway between the aft cabin and the main saloon."

"This will create real suffering for the grandparent who has to visit the head at night," said John.

"Covered, my love," I said. "We'll keep a bucket in the aft cabin."

"So where do we put Rupert if he comes to visit?" John asked.

"Well," I said, "Rupert's not talking to either John Jr. or Lisa, so he'll want to stay in a motel. Paul is very fond of Rupert, so Rupert can take him swimming. Lito and John Jr. like each other, and Lisa and I can visit because I'm still mad at John Jr. over that speeding ticket, and the kitten can entertain himself."

"So who do I visit with?" asked John.

"Mikey," I said.

"Mikey doesn't speak English," said John.

"But you do, my love," I said soothingly. "Think how much he'll learn from his granddad. You can teach him his first words — 'radar', 'GPS', and 'power tools.'"

"There's something in that," John admitted. "But how can you find the true meaning of Christmas on board a boat? There's no room."

"You forget, darling," I said happily. "The very first Christmas had a baby and a problem with overcrowding."

"Why, so it did," said John reflectively. "So it did."

May the Christmas season be filled with blessings for you and all your family.

High Fashion on the Docks

HAVE YOU EVER noticed that a high-fashion runway is shaped exactly like a dock? There are mornings when I make my straddle-legged way down a heaving dock with my purse strap wrapped around my neck and clenched in my teeth for extra safekeeping and both arms extended for balance, when I feel as though I, too, am making a fashion statement — one for which there are mercifully no witnesses.

The Cowichan Bay fashion model can't slip one hand casually into a pocket as she struts down the dock in case her hand closes on her keys and she loses both her balance and the keys in the same graceful arcing motion. Stiletto heels are out of the question — she must wear flats with a solid all-weather rubber tread, appropriate for snow, frost, sleet, rain and other adverse dock conditions. She wants something that will grip as she wields a snow shovel, yet look stylish at dock parties. This narrows it down to the common sneaker — appropriate for all social occasions at Cowichan Bay. The Cowichan Bay model is not a shrivelled anorexia victim — she is muscular and hearty, capable of cleaning out bilges and swabbing decks. She doesn't have the intent, serious expression of a Paris runway model —

she is a woman capable of seeing humour in the situation when her husband spends their last dollar on a hammer drill to make holes in the deck.

Voluminous skirts are out of the question. The Cowichan Bay model needs both hands to balance — not control her skirts in a stiff breeze. Sheath skirts are unbecoming as the model straddles the dock, and don't go well with sneakers. Dresses are not usually seen on the docks, in case the wearer has to crawl into a small space or clean something musty. Slacks are the clothing of choice, but fancy dry-cleanable fabrics are impractical. This limits the field to blue jeans, which are worn by everyone without regard to gender, age, marital status or weight. They must not be too tight, in case the model falls off the dock and has to swim to safety or yell for help, and not too new, in case her neighbours laugh at her. Cowichan Bay blue jeans are neither designer blue jeans, nor freshly pressed and laundered. They have the casual, relaxed air of jeans that have been worn while doing chores. We call it "mildew chic."

The Cowichan Bay model, striding confidently down the dock or crawling on her hands and knees over two boards lashed together, gives some thought to her accessories. Many a local woman has been spotted with a wheelbarrow filled with gallon containers of diesel fuel. Gunmetal grey is the colour of choice for this accessory, and though the variation in styles is limited, this remains a popular item. A snow shovel is another seasonal accessory no woman would want to be seen without. Slung casually by one hand and ready for instant use, the snow shovel is a woman's best friend for winter and greatly enhances her attractiveness in the eyes of the local men, many of whom jocularly offer little tips on how her shovelling performance could be improved. These instructions are received with the characteristic graceful graciousness one expects from the Cowichan Bay woman. "Bugger off," she says.

A flashlight can be both attractive and functional. Cowichan Bay models prefer the matte finish of plastic or the glamorous shimmer of aluminum. A heavy flashlight can be useful for repelling boarders, fighting off vicious animals and providing ballast.

Purses are slung casually around the neck, leaving both hands free to haul bags of garbage to the disposal unit on the way to work.

Differing dock conditions demand variations in the walking style. For example, there is a model's walk peculiar to the hauling of garbage. The arms are stiffly extended to either side and the step increases in caution, toes first. The model with garbage has the right-of-way on the dock. Snow, and the model is bent over double in "shovel" position. Ice, and she spreads her legs astraddle and waddles cautiously down the dock with her arms extended. Rain, she bows her head and hurries. Sleet, she stays on board. A heaving dock demands certain skills of the model. She must venture down the dock in "ready to fall off the dock" position, as cautiously as Indiana Jones entering the Temple of Doom. Yes, we're as versatile as movie stars, the women of Cowichan Bay.

Certainly, one of the reasons why our husbands find us so attractive, as we make our way down the dock, is that most of us have jobs. We don't get paid for our glamorous and chic appearance, but we do get paid. Cindy Crawford, eat your heart out!

Books On Board

"LOVE ME, LOVE my 300 pounds of books," I told John. "But do they all have to be on board?" moaned my long-suffering husband.

"Throw the EPIRB overboard and bring on a copy of *Moby Dick*," I said. "I'm not sailing anywhere without the complete Charles Dickens, the complete Jane Austen and everything Mary Renault ever wrote. We can't go to the South Seas without Joseph Conrad, darling. How would we know how to deal with discontented colonials and the conflicts deep within our own hearts? Peggotty, uncle of *David Copperfield,* was a live-aboard, the hero in Jane Austen's *Persuasion* was a sailor — a captain, no less — and all of Mary Renault's heroes were Greeks, so they knew how to swim in the ocean. King Arthur, in the third volume of Mary Stewart's masterpiece, was cast adrift on a boat surrounded by weeping women — I'd weep too if I had to sit in a leaky old barge of that era — and Sinbad of my Penguin collection of *Arabian Tales* was the quintessential adventurer and an inspiration to us all.

"The mindless optimism of Voltaire's *Candide* is not unlike the state of mind of the average sailor — happiness near akin to mental illness in the face of one disaster after another. His disasters were social and ours are mechanical, but no matter. The message is the same. There's something wrong with us, but we're happy.

"I need my copies of *I Claudius* and *Claudius the God.* You never know, but we may meet some Italian sailors in our travels, and we'll want something to talk about. Besides, didn't Claudius conduct a brilliant campaign by sea against Great Britain? He has tips for transporting camels and elephants we may find helpful. *The Five Little Peppers* could cook using all substituted ingredients on primitive equipment — just like our diesel oven, darling, and my collection of pioneer cookbook reprints has lots of useful suggestions on how to work around a lack of refrigeration. The pioneers couldn't imagine refrigeration and after a year on board the *Inuksuk* I've forgotten it.

"The possibilities for learning about sailing from great literature are endless. When I was ten, I memorized all 625 lines of *The Rime of the Ancient Mariner* — I notice you've avoided having me recite them to you — but darling, you'll never catch me aiming the flare gun at an albatross. As for 'The Wreck of the Hesperus,' I could tell right away the skipper's daughter showing her bosom in an ice storm was wearing improper gear. Do our masts float, by the way? And do I get to be tied to one of them if it gets rough?

"If we go offshore, we'll need P.G. Wodehouse's perfect butler Jeeves to remind us of how to live graciously, and Rumpole has all manner of legal advice and insight into the criminal mind. We may encounter pirates, after all. Margaret Laurence will remind us of what we left behind in Canada, and draw us unerringly home again. It's lucky I'm well-read, darling. Any emergency marine situation we find ourselves in, we can just start reading through my three-hundred pounds of books. Aren't you glad one of us knows how to do research?"

Don't Try This at Home!

WE FOUND THE ad in *The Boat Journal.* My husband and I ended up staggering around Vancouver dragging a secondhand four-man life raft we could barely lift between us.

"A real bargain," said John enthusiastically.

I heaved one end of the life raft by the frayed rope wrapped around it.

"Are there four freeze-dried men in here?" I asked. "It's too heavy to take across on the ferry as freight — we'll have to carry it on as hand luggage."

We made the first ferry from Gibsons, but missed the second and I ended up sitting on a park bench at Horseshoe Bay watching the last ferry of the night pull rapidly away from us. Some women go dancing. Some women go out for dinner. I sat on a park bench drinking tea I'd bought at a garage, knitting socks in the dark, and guarding the life raft — as if anyone could lift it to steal it anyway – while my husband agonized over whether to call a cab or wait for our son-in-law to fix his car. At 10:30 PM he gave up and we hailed a cab.

Day two of our saga found us sleeping on a mattress on the floor at daughter Maggie's apartment. At 6:30 AM John sprang out of bed.

"We don't want to miss the first ferry," he said.

I rolled onto the floor and lay on my back. My entire body hurt.

"We spent all our money on the cab last night," said John. "So we'll have to get back to Horseshoe Bay by SkyTrain and bus."

I moaned and opened one eye. There was not a pleasant look in it. "Coffee," I croaked. "Coffee or I die." Then I rolled over onto my hands and knees and crawled to the washroom.

I shall draw a merciful curtain of oblivion over the pain and agony of the rest of the trip. Suffice to say that as I lay collapsed in my seat on the ferry, I gave some thought to dialling 911 on my cell phone and requesting a helicopter to airlift me out of my chair and into a waiting ambulance, leaving the life raft behind me. But my husband uttered words of encouragement.

"Rouse yourself, my little dumpling. This life raft cost us eight hundred and fifty dollars. I'd as soon leave you behind."

So instead, I hauled my share of it through miles of corridors at Departure Bay, and then I draped myself over top of the life raft in the drop-off area and waited for John to come with the car. Idly, I opened the survival manual that came with the life raft and perused the pages. One line jumped out at me: "All seabirds are edible." I sat up in excitement.

I recalled a story my husband had told me about Great Whale River in Canada's Arctic about forty years ago. He'd been invited to a community feast put on by an independent fur trader who had been run out of business by the Hudson's Bay Company. Just before he went broke he threw a party and invited everyone he knew who didn't work for the Bay. John qualified. He'd been fired from the Hudson's Bay Company for "fraternizing with the natives" when he'd married Louise, who was Inuit. The host promised homebrew, bannock and stew, and the crowd was not disappointed. There were stacks of bannock, gallons of homebrew and, bubbling in a forty-five-gallon drum, the stew. The host had neglected to mention what the stew was made of. Seagulls. Forty-five gallons of seagull stew.

The party was a hit. John reports that the stew was somewhat fishy, but after the second tin mug of homebrew nobody complained. The entire community jigged the night away and rolled home in the wee hours, satiated and tipsy. I bet the Hudson's Bay Company manager was seething with jealousy.

When John returned with the car, I pressed him for details. What, I wanted to know, was in the seagull stew of so many years ago? John stared at me incredulously.

"Potatoes and onions, I think. You're not going to WRITE about it?"

"Absolutely not, darling," I said.

So I won't.

But flexibility is an important characteristic of the mariner, and the first mate. Between us, our combination of ingenuity, physical strength and good sportsmanship will stand us in good stead. Should we ever have to use the life raft, however, it does not bode well for the friendly seagull.

The Albatross

"'It is an ancient mariner,'" I chanted.

"No! No! Anything but poetry," my husband gasped. "Turn on the TV! Do you want to go for a walk? Buy ice cream? Go for a row in the dinghy?"

"'And he stoppeth one of three,'" I said.

"'By thy long grey beard and glittering eye,
Now wherefore stopp'st thou me?'"

"I surrender," John said. "Unconditionally. You may have anything you like, even half my kingdom and a trip to Value Village."

"Well, it's a tempting offer," I said, "but really, all I want is a few chores done around the boat.

'Water water everywhere
and all the boards did shrink;
Water water everywhere.
Nor any drop to drink. The very deep did rot…'"

"Stop! Stop!" John begged. "I'm leaving to fill the water tanks. Honestly. Right now. And I'll clean the bilge too — it's getting kind of dieselly down there. The diesel stove carburetor isn't leaking too badly, though."

"'And I have done a hellish thing,

And it would work 'em woe
For all averred, I had killed the bird
That made the breeze to blow.'"
"Oh, all right, I'll fix the carburetor. And do the laundry. Do
you want anything done on the car?"
"'I looked upon the rotting sea
And drew my eyes away
I looked upon the rotting deck
And there the dead men lay.'"
"I'll scrub the deck too if you like. Just stop reciting
poetry. Please."

I sighed with happiness. Our neighbour says there is a direct
correlation between menopause and boat maintenance. Her
husband is out in all weathers fixing the boat, she says, because
he's too frightened to come on board. But who would have
thought that poetry would have the same awesome power as
hormonal fluctuations?

As John fled up the ladder to fill the water tanks, I sat down
excitedly to make a list of more chores. *The Rime of the Ancient
Mariner* is a very long poem, and I should be able to get a lot
of nautical mileage out of it. I looked happily around the main
saloon. The teak needed oiling, and the brass polishing. The
books had to be straightened, the engine oil needed changing,
and several of our bilge compartments needed scrubbing. I sus-
pected the little stainless steel water tank had a slow leak —
someone would have to drain it and then time the number of
seconds the bilge alarm went off in a day. Or was the bilge hose
cracked?

The flashlight I used for looking in the hanging lockers needed batteries, and one of us would have to turn off the diesel

oven and take a palm sander to the stovetop. It was starting to look grungy. The hose connections in the bilge could use a little Sikoflex. Now that the winter rains had let up it was getting to be the time of year to wipe down the lockers with vinegar, and wash and put away our winter clothing, and wash and iron our summer wardrobes. I thought with a sigh of John's favourite shorts, resplendent with paint stains and dyed the most ghastly shade of orangey-brown known to man. A triumph of ugliness, they had survived the four summers of our marriage: four haul-outs with the neighbours watching.

I bet the head could do with a conditioning treatment, not to mention a cleaning in all those impossible corners. How old was John's toothbrush? Was the day fuel tank full? I jumped up to check the gauge. It wouldn't hurt to take a look at the rigging. We should get our hands on a bosun's chair and go up the mast. The loudspeaker for the hailer system had been dangling for a month.

And the zincs should be checked. There's a lot of electrolysis in Cowichan Bay, and we put zincs on during our last haul-out, over half a year ago. John should repair that little outboard engine. The dinghy was looking a little soft. Were the lamps all full of lamp oil? The freezer was shot, and we should find another repairman. The last one who'd been recommended to us had been taken away in handcuffs before he could lay one finger on our freezer. The tinned-goods locker was dwindling and we were out of light bulbs.

John came down the companionway ladder and bent over the water tank valves with a flashlight.

"Darling," I said.

"Yes?" said John.

"I have here a list of twenty-seven chores that have to be done, and I haven't even touched the summer haul-out of the car. How did we leave the mortgage-dragging, haggard-faced land-dwelling life behind us, only to come to this day, on this boat, surrounded by this much maintenance?"

"I never promised you a rose garden," said John. "I promised you a boat."

I sighed. "I never thought it would be this much work. I fantasized carefree sails around the bay, crabpot fishing by moonlight, and strolls down the dock with the man I love. Instead we got towed by moonlight, we dodged crabpots in the bay, and I crawled over the docks on my hands and knees while you held the flashlight so I could see where the docks had broken up."

"That was the fun part," said John. "Help me with these valves?"

"The ancient mariner put to sea to get away from boat maintenance," I said. "That was really the albatross around his neck."

John turned some valves, then listened for the water to gurgle into the first tank. "He couldn't have been very good at it. Didn't his boat sink?"

"'The ship went down like lead,'" I quoted glumly.

"A sailor is a carefree lad," said John. "Let me share with you my philosophy of life: Relax. Try not to get fired. Live on a boat."

"Then I'll quote my last quote," I said.

"'Then from my neck so free,
The albatross fell off and sank like lead into the sea.'"

"Let's ditch this albatross and go sailing," said John. "But no more poetry."

"Of course not, my darling," I said. "Instead, how about I sing to you?"